THE FEAR OF GOD

THE FEAR OF GOD

The Role of Anxiety in Contemporary Thought

by
Fred Berthold, Jr.

HARPER & BROTHERS PUBLISHERS NEW YORK

To my parents

THE FEAR OF GOD
Copyright © 1959 by Fred Berthold, Jr.
Printed in the United States of America

H-I

Library of Congress catalog card number: 59-10329

Contents

Preface

The views expressed in the following pages were developed over a period of almost fifteen years. I wish to acknowledge my indebtedness to my seminary teachers at The University of Chicago, particularly to Professor Daniel Day Williams, now of Union Theological Seminary in New York City. During my years as a teacher at Dartmouth College, a number of colleagues have stimulated and admonished me in an endless process of friendly debate. In particular, Professor Maurice Mandelbaum, now at Johns Hopkins University, forced me again and again, by virtue of his naturalistic position and his generous concern for the development of my own views, to rethink my own assumptions and methods. From my undergraduate days and continuing to the present, the insights and friendship of Professor Francis W. Gramlich have been of great importance to me. I also wish to thank Professor T. S. K. Scott-Craig, whose theological wisdom has inspired and often corrected me; and my wife, whom I met as a fellow student of theology and who has been a constant support and companion in theology as well as in life generally.

My very special and heartfelt thanks go to the trustees of The George A. and Eliza Gardner Howard Foundation. A generous grant from this foundation permitted me the leisure to complete my manuscript.

While I am indebted to all of these, and to others as well, I must accept personal responsibility for whatever defects may appear in the following presentation.

F. B.

Dartmouth College
Hanover, New Hampshire
June 1, 1959

I

The Present Situation in Theology

INTRODUCTION

Occasionally a friend has sought to save me from the folly of taking a serious interest in theology. More than once the old joke has been quoted to me: theology is a midnight search in an unlighted cellar for a black cat that isn't there. I had always assumed that this joke was originated by someone hostile to theology; but, after reading in recent continental theology, I am no longer certain of that. It seems now to be the fashion for theologians to admit, and even to glory in, the futility of theology—at least insofar as theology is thought of as a human search.

We are told that the human situation is that we do *not* know God. We are separated from God by an impassable gulf. Any effort of ours to bridge the gulf only witnesses to our demonic pride, only puts us in touch with gods of our own making whose function it is to reflect and "secure" our own selfish desires. Man is, indeed, in the dark. And he gropes for cats that he persists in believing are there.

The first function of true theology, as against this merely human groping, is, we are told, to pronounce that we do not find God. Then and only then can true theology go on to witness to the fact that God has found us.

This, it seems to me, is the mood of much theology today. It is the mood of self-criticism, or even self-castigation. Such a mood is no doubt an inevitable and, in many

ways, salutary reaction to the buoyant hopes and lofty claims
of "liberal theology." Liberal theology boasted not merely a
lot of knowledge about God but even a familiar and almost
cozy relàtionship with Him. Disillusionment with such a
view was perhaps brought on by the course of practical af-
fairs—I mean by the shipwreck of our hopes for universal
peace and democracy. But the practical impetus to abandon
the hopes of liberalism was matched by powerful developments in modern thought. The influence of both existentialism and positivism has grown, and both are acutely aware
of the limitations of thought. The climate has grown un-
friendly to any kind of metaphysical thinking and in particular to any claims of rational knowledge of God.

Much recent theology, like most philosophy in the modern period, has been dominated by the problem of knowledge. But the feeling of a gulf between man and God is
not confined to the sphere of knowledge. It tends to spread
to every department of theology and to suggest an absolute
gulf also in the sphere of "being." Along with the agnos-
ticism of recent continental theology goes an assertion that
man as a total being is radically separated from God. Man
is lost, derelict, alone, condemned to nothingness.

I have been moved to write what follows for a number of
reasons—for example, because I find the inquiry into the
significance of religious anxiety interesting in its own right.
But, also, I feel that this inquiry may provide a perspective
from which the pronouncement of man's total depravity
and separation from God may be critically viewed. In fact,
my interest in the problem of anxiety sprang from the feeling that, on the one hand, certain theologians tended to cite
the anxiety of man as evidence of his separation from God
and, on the other hand, that a more penetrating examination of the evidence would not support this interpretation.

We are perhaps most of all indebted to the existentialists
for the suggestion that man's anxiety reveals something fun-

damental about the human situation. And there can be no doubt that continental theology has been profoundly influenced by existentialism. It is easy to get the impression, perhaps especially from Heidegger and Sartre, that what anxiety reveals about man is simply his "nothingness." But I have become convinced that such a reading of their testimony is mistaken. Furthermore, this negative appraisal of anxiety is even more doubtful when we bring into view the actual experience of religious anxiety and the understanding of anxiety made available to us by other serious students of its nature.

But if the negative appraisal of anxiety cannot be supported, as I shall try to show, we are still faced with the question: What does man's anxiety signify concerning his fundamental situation and his relation to God?

I cannot claim to have produced a final answer to this question, much less one which is beyond debate. But I hope that I have been able to open new channels of conversation on the matter. This hope is the only excuse for yet another book on anxiety. It marks off my effort from the many excellent but primarily practical and pastoral treatments of the subject. My intention is to enter the realm of constructive theological thought through this particular topic.

ANXIETY AND THE DESIRE FOR GOD

Suppose that Martin Heidegger is right in feeling that the phenomenon of anxiety provides one of the best clues for understanding man and his relation to whatever is ultimately most real. What are we to make of those anxieties which reflect a religious context and concern?

When religious anxiety is spoken of, one's thoughts turn first, no doubt, to such black and foreboding states as fear of death, or anguish over guilt, or an overwhelming feeling of one's nothingness. In considering religious anxiety, should we omit reference to such an experience as Bunyan reports in the case of two pilgrims nearing Heaven?

. . . by reason of the natural glory of the city and the reflection of the sunbeams upon it, Christian with desire fell sick. Hopeful also had a fit or two of the same disease. Wherefore they lay by it a while, crying out because of their pangs, "If you see my Beloved, tell him that I am sick of love." [1]

I shall seek to show, by an analysis of the experience of anxiety, that such an "anxiety of desire" is by no means to be ignored; that, in fact, it is fundamental in the whole phenomenon of anxiety. My theme, in brief, is that anxiety is a profoundly polar or ambivalent thing. It is true that its blacker aspects may often be to the fore in our conscious awareness. But analysis discloses that they always presuppose a positive desire. In the religious context, anxiety over death, guilt, and the like are grounded upon a desire for God. To use Bunyan's word, anxiety is a phenomenon of "love"—to be sure, of love that is threatened but of love nonetheless.

If such is the case, can we not draw out certain implications for theology? Common sense might seem to suggest the following conclusion: even the finite, sinful man is not without a striving toward God. Man is not completely fallen, separated from God. For is there not a desire for God implicit even in our worst fears of separation from Him, of judgment by Him, and even in our painful sense of nothingness? This common-sense conclusion reminds us to some extent of the time-honored scholastic doctrine of man's natural desire for God, a doctrine which I will want to discuss later (see pp. 78 ff.). As most laymen realize, however, theology is by no means identical with common sense. In particular, it would seem to be overly naïve to leap to the suggested conclusion in view of the present theological situation. One cannot ignore the weighty criticisms of a simple appeal to religious experience as the source of theology.

THE APPEAL TO RELIGIOUS EXPERIENCE

In modern times, it seems to me, religious experience has been regarded by theologians in three quite different fundamental ways.

Liberalism. It is not too much to say that theology entered its modern phase with the work of that thinker who made the appeal to religious experience the basis for all doctrine, that is, with the work of F. D. E. Schleiermacher. Following his lead, theological liberalism found its greatest tool for liberating men from the past in the notion that present experience is the criterion for faith. Whether, for example, Schleiermacher reduced "God" to a mode of human consciousness is still discussed. However this may be, there can be no doubt that he turned away from the historical basis of Christianity.

The profound tendency in Schleiermacher to psychologize theology may be seen in his distinction between the three "dogmatic forms." The first form consists of statements about the religious self-consciousness itself; the second about God; the third about the world. In principle, says Schleiermacher, statements of the second and third forms may be eliminated, or reduced to statements of the first form.

My concentration upon the phenomena of religious anxiety falls within the first form, according to the classification of Schleiermacher. Does this commit me to the rest of his program? Not at all. For, as I shall seek to show (see Chapter VII), one may take religious experience seriously, as being of importance to theology, without holding that theological statements may be inductively established on the basis of the analysis of such experience. The relationship between experience and theology is more complex than Schleiermacher realized.

Karl Barth. There are many ways in which one might approach Barth's attitude toward the relation of religious experience to theology. This whole matter will be dealt with

more fully later (Chapter VIII), but it will be helpful at
this juncture of preliminary orientation to be aware of the
main direction of his thinking. Barth was by no means the
first to protest against Schleiermacher's program. Franz
Overbeck in his *Christentum und Kultur*[2] argued that
Schleiermacher was able to tell us of nothing except "the
poor little rags with which man cloaks his religion." The
theologian tells us and can tell us nothing of God or the soul
but only of human experience. According to Overbeck,
Schleiermacher's attempt to evolve a theology from a "feeling of dependence" is reminiscent of the Epicurean attempt
to trace religion back to "fear of the gods." From such a
starting point, the atheism of the Epicureans is just as legi-
timate a conclusion as those at which Schleiermacher ar-
rives.

However, in our day Barth is the outstanding and representative spokesman of those who reject the program of
basing theology upon religious experience. His attitude can
be seen most easily, perhaps, in a lecture which he delivered
on Feuerbach, which has now been translated by James
Luther Adams as the Introduction to Feuerbach's *The Essence of Christianity*.[3] Here Barth discusses Feuerbach's contention that the real essence of Christianity is the divinity
of man. God is the essence of man, the essence which man
is struggling to realize. Barth says that Feuerbach's contention is absolutely unanswerable by any theology based upon
an analysis of the experience of man. "Whoever is concerned with the spirit, the heart, and conscience and the
inwardness of man must be confronted with the question of
whether he is really concerned with God and not with the
apotheosis of man." We must be capable of admitting "to
Feuerbach that he is entirely right in his interpretation of
religion insofar as it relates not only to religion as an experience of evil in mortal man but also to the high, the ponder-
able and even the Christian religion of this man. Are we
willing to admit that even in our relation to God we are and

remain liars and that we can lay claim to his truth, his certainty, his salvation as grace and only as grace? . . . So long as the talk about 'God and man' is not cut out at the roots, we have no cause to criticize Feuerbach." [4]

Barth contends, then, that an analysis of religious experience tells us only about man, not about God. It may, indeed, speak of "God," but this God is only a symbol for our own ideals or values. There is no way from our imminent experiences to the transcendent God.

The rejection of religious experience as a basis for theology need not mean that one is disinterested in it. Barth makes this plain in his treatment of Schleiermacher. [5] But, as Barth understands it, we can include our study of man and all the varieties of his experience only as they are seen in the light of the Word of God. The meaning of the Word of God is not established by an analysis of experience. The Word of God, by grace, creates within us its own meaning, and in its light we may then rightly understand our experience.

Personally I do not feel that I can accept Barth's view of the relation of religious experience to theology, even though his protest has helped to overcome the dangers of Schleiermacher's view. Obviously, before I am through, I will have to state my own view on this issue (see Chapter VII). But now I only want to point out that in the light of the present situation in theology, as I see it, a new approach to this question is called for. Barth has cut the ground out from under the liberal, "scientific" appropriation of religious experience. But in his turn he robs it of any independent value for theology. If Schleiermacher psychologized theology, Barth theologizes everything.

Rudolf Bultmann. From the point of view of our problem, the work of Rudolf Bultmann represents an awareness of the need for a new approach as well as a contribution to it. Bultmann is well aware that the task which he sets himself of an "existential interpretation" of Scripture and of theology is not easy; that it will require the effort of a whole theological generation. It is not to be wondered, therefore, that clarity is lacking at many points as to the meaning of Bultmann's categories and methods. What I want to point out here is simply this: he calls for an advance beyond both Schleiermacher and Barth. With this I am in full agreement and will have to return to Bultmann when discussing more fully what this might involve. A new effort is called for. I shall offer my suggestions along this line after making the analysis of religious anxiety, using this analysis as a constant point of reference.

THE IMAGE OF GOD

I do not wish, however, to give the impression that I will be concerned only with methodological matters. The phenomenon of man's anxious desire for God has a bearing also upon vital doctrinal matters. In particular, I believe that an understanding of this phenomenon may help to shed light upon some of the ancient theological debates on "the image of God." Has the image been lost in the Fall? Does sinful man still in some sense seek God? I hope that my analysis of religious anxiety will provide me with categories of interpretation which may make it possible to approach this matter in a somewhat new and helpful way.

A COMMENT ON SIGMUND FREUD

That religious experience may be of interest to theology has been challenged from quite a different quarter, too—from the point of view of depth psychology. Freud, and many of his followers, have sought to assimilate religious experience to the realm of the neurotic mental life. Freud viewed religion as a kind of compulsive neurosis which, however, was not generally so regarded because of its wide acceptance in society. Very much interested in religious experience, Freud felt that he was capable of explaining it in a way that destroys the very foundations of theology. God was "explained" as a projection of our attitudes toward our human fathers, especially in their roles as authorities who enforce moral sanctions. Similarly, he felt that other concepts which arise in religious experience refer to the psychic life of the individual in his social relations and not to any transcendent Being. Freud would agree with Barth: religious experience gives testimony only to man's nature and not to God's nature.

It is important at the outset for me to make clear how I will view the psychoanalytic approach to religious experience, so far as this work is concerned. For there will seem to be many points at which it would be relevant but at which I have not referred to it. For example, some of the experiences which Teresa of Ávila reports (see the one cited on pp. 34-35 below) and some of the language she uses seem to cry for psychoanalytic interpretation. Interpretations of this kind have been offered by others. I do not wish at all to deny that the concepts of sexual frustration and repression, or of hysteria, and the like, are probably applicable in this case—though it should be remembered that historical records do not afford a very reliable basis for an interpretation of such personal experiences.

I have sought elsewhere, however, to draw a distinction between the *meaning* of such experiences and their metaphysical or ontological *explanation*.[6] Before judging the truth of the explanation which is offered to account for any experience, it is important to see what the experience means to the one who has it. In terms of the meaning of Teresa's experience, we must speak of such things as "the desire for God." When we ask for an explanation, we may discuss whether there is, in fact, a God of whom she has had experience, or whether she is simply projecting some inner, psychic struggle, or what not. These latter questions, however, are not psychological questions but ontological questions. I refer the reader to my article for my argument that the psychologist, as a psychologist, has no special competence to judge the ontological status of the objects referred to in experience. If he does so, it is either as a philosopher (meta-physician) or on the basis of "common sense" assumptions which often are not critically examined.

It is not to be denied that many religious people give evidence that their religious experiences and concepts are related to the kinds of psychic traumas and deprivations which make it plausible to attempt a psychoanalytic explanation. Some aspects of mystical experiences, for example, remind one of certain neurotic symptoms. In terms of the distinction which I am urging, however, we may recall the contention of William James: that an individual may be psychically unbalanced, or neurotic, and still genuinely aware of religious realities.[7] James even suggests that some disturbances may help an individual to a more sensitive awareness. The reality of an object of belief is not to be judged on the basis of the way in which that belief functions in the dynamic structure of psychic life.

What does this mean for our attitude toward Freud in this particular work? It means that we may recognize his value so far as he illuminates the psychological processes of any human experience, including religious experience. Actually Freud's understanding of the dynamics of anxiety is of immense value to us; *for he shows anxiety to have the very same psychological structure as that which emerges from our study of religious anxiety.* But here we must draw a line. When it comes to the question of the reality of the objects toward which, or before which, this anxiety is displayed, we must go beyond what Freud as a psychologist can tell us. So far as the analysis of experience reveals, Teresa's anxiety is in relation to God. I am very much concerned to show that this anxiety, as it is understood by Teresa herself, displays the same psychological dynamics as those anxieties analyzed by Freud. But is her anxiety *really* in relation to God? This question cannot be answered by any description of psychological processes.

As a matter of fact, I must refrain in this work from trying to settle the metaphysical question: Is there *really* a *God* before whom man is anxious? Such an attempt would, to put it mildly, be quite an undertaking. My analysis will take place within the context of theology. This means that the reality of God is assumed. The question for debate, on the basis of the analysis of certain kinds of religious experience, is not "Is there a God?" but "What concept of the relation of God and man is consistent with the experience we have?"

II

The Way of Fear:

ANXIETY IN TERESA OF ÁVILA

People of all persuasions who have taken the trouble to get acquainted with Teresa of Ávila have come to understand why she is a saint "that moved the world." [1] Some have been moved primarily by her soaring, indomitable spiritual imagination; others, by her earthy common sense. Among the mystics she ranks with those of the most powerful inner vision and the most compelling sense of divine calling. Among those of practical genius she ranks as a master organizer and maker of history with whom kings and princes had to reckon. The Reformed Order of Carmel, which she founded, stands as a living testimony both to the power of her love of God and to the depth of her understanding of man. The mystical bride of Christ, she was also the eagle-eyed prioress who detected the least bit of shoddy work by the masons who built her convent walls or the careless dropping of a knitting stitch by one of her spiritual daughters—and who dealt firmly but with high good humor with each. Transported by mystical raptures, she could yet joke with her daughters about the silly, female weaknesses which so often disguised themselves as movements of the divine spirit. Her spirit was supple; yet it was strong. Beset by fears and doubts which suggest, to the modern mind, a neurotic streak, she yet conveys the impression of a fundamental integrity and common sense which many a "sane" person should be happy to possess.

As a mystic, Teresa was concerned with the various "ways" by which the human spirit might come into union with God. In one striking passage of her autobiography, Teresa says of herself that she was being led "by the way of fear." [2] Almost everything that Teresa wrote is profoundly autobiographical, though not always explicitly so; and this characterization of her "way" as the "way of fear" is richly adumbrated. Indeed, so rich is the material which might be brought to bear upon this theme that space will permit not even a summary of it all. It will be necessary to concentrate upon a few outstanding modes of this fear. Those which are selected are those which stand out in Teresa's own understanding of her life, and which assume a permanent importance in her fully developed and characteristic piety.[3]

The relative lack of reference in what follows to the everyday anxieties which are the common lot of mankind does not mean that I wish to disguise the fact that Teresa suffered from them. Indeed, I would insist that she exhibits these more than is commonly the case. She was a sensitive and scrupulous person. Her protestations of love for her father, undoubtedly sincere, cannot hide the fact that she feared him on account of his moralistic severity. Though treated in a delicate and obscure way, an adolescent romantic upheaval is evident. Over this she suffered a considerable sense of guilt, heightened by fear that her father would discover her "vanity."

Furthermore, at the height of these youthful tempests, when Teresa was fourteen years old, her mother died. Though Teresa does not speak much of her mother, she evidently enjoyed a close and sympathetic relation with her. Together they had often read secretly, for fear of the father's displeasure, books of chivalry and romance. It is said, though it cannot be proven, that the young Teresa herself wrote a book of chivalric romance. In any case, something of the flavor of the *hidalgo* conquest is to be seen in all her later assaults upon Heaven. When her mother died, Teresa was frightened and bewildered, and she pleaded tearfully with St. Anne to become her mother.

If I were interested in establishing whether Teresa was or was not a neurotic (perhaps a victim of hysteria as Leuba insists),[4] it would be necessary to dwell upon such matters at great length. For my part, I am willing to accept as probably correct the judgment that Teresa was neurotic. It no doubt brings joy to the Freudian heart that much evidence, supplied by Teresa herself, can be cited to support the view that her disturbances were related to sexual frustrations. On the other hand, there is a good deal of evidence to suggest that Teresa was, as a child, fundamentally happy and outgoing. She was apparently well liked and was something of a natural leader. For reasons given above, I shall regard such questions as lying outside the scope of this inquiry. I am interested in the structure of her anxieties as they appear in the religious context and as they are represented in Teresa's own self-understanding.

Desire for Eternal Life

The first anxiety which appeared in her life was of a positive kind. We sometimes use the term "anxious" in phrases containing "anxious to . . ." and sometimes in phrases containing "anxious about . . ." I must insist at this point that we not direct out attention exclusively to the latter. For my essential thesis is that, in ways to be explained, the two sides are always linked together.

This first anxiety of which I speak was an anxiety to find and enjoy eternity. Teresa became conscious of this desire very early in her life, and it stayed with her as an overtone to all her later anxieties. With a kind of ecstatic fervor Teresa and her favorite brother Rodrigo used to repeat the word "Forever! Forever!" At her suggestion the six-year-old Teresa and her ten-year-old brother started down the road one day "to the land of the Moors." They knew only that it lay to the south. They expected that once there they would be beheaded for their faith and would be immediately raised to eternal heavenly bliss. The two "knights" were, however, discovered by an uncle only a short distance from Ávila and were returned home by him. Frustrated in her ambition but still fascinated by eternity, Teresa organized her playmates into "monasteries" and "convents" where her hopes could be realized, she felt, in another way.[5]

This episode smacks, no doubt, of the chivalry which occupied her imagination, and of religious notions which were quite conventional in her milieu. Yet it is quite consistent with her later life. Even as a mature nun, her drive toward perfection is suggestive of high adventure. In that age, it was perhaps the only adventure which was realistic for a woman. However much her later reactions appear to be dominated by fearful and constrictive anxieties, she retained the sense of being called onward by something intrinsically and overpoweringly desirable: by perfection, by eternity. This early experience should be recalled when we come later to describe the distinctive Teresian anxiety, which can only be called an anxiety of desire.

ANXIETY OVER DEATH AND SIN

It was not long, however, before this youthful fascination was beclouded by an anxiety which was for Teresa terribly frightening, namely, anxiety about death and Hell. Religious hope and desire seemed for some time to be overwhelmed by fear. Why should Teresa, who at one time sought death, now fear it? Because she was now convinced of her sin and afraid that death would bring her into Hell. The anxiety about sin and guilt became intense just at the time of her adolescent vanities. She feared her father's wrath and, also, the wrath of her Father in Heaven. And this fear remained with Teresa almost to the end of her days, if not to the very end. I shall not attempt a complete catalogue of these black states. Suffice it to say that Teresa

can vie with almost any deeply religious person of those
times for honors in morbid scrupulosity. She was sure that
her vanities (perhaps an innocent romantic flirtation) merited Hell. She believed that she was worthy of damnation
because, as a nun in her earlier years, she wasted time in
the convent parlor in idle gossip with friends from outside.
Teresa undertook severe mortifications in an attempt to as-
suage these assaults of guilty anxiety. And in the process she
ruined her health, indeed almost died.

Teresa reports that her decision to become a nun is related to this anxiety of guilt and fear of Hell. When she
was fifteen or sixteen years of age, her father placed her
in an Augustinian convent. He was apparently afraid that
he could not manage his attractive and volatile daughter,
now that her mother was dead. And he no doubt had some
inkling of her vanities. In any case, it took Teresa only a
short time to ruin her health. Driven by feelings of her sin-
fulness, she undertook excessive self-discipline. She even
prayed for suffering. Soon her health gave way, and she was
removed from the convent by her father.

After some time of convalescence, Teresa became worried
about her destiny. She argued that, being so sinful, she
merited Hell. But she felt that if she could force herself
to become a nun and mortify herself in this life, she might
escape this terrible end and enjoy eternal life. Teresa reports her state of mind:

I used to try to convince myself by using the following argument. The trials and distresses of being a nun could not be
greater than those of purgatory and I had fully deserved to be
in Hell. It would not be a great matter to spend my life as
though I were in purgatory if afterwards I were to go straight to
Heaven, which was what I desired. *This decision then, to enter
the religious life seems to have been inspired by servile fear
more than by love.*[6]

We can reckon that a period of six or seven years was

dominated by a deep conflict connected with entering the religious life. During this period Teresa's anxieties reach one of the high peaks of her life. And at this time three aspects of anxiety are closely correlated: anxiety over death and Hell, anxiety over guilt, and a definite set of physical symptoms of anxiety. The connection between these elements is suggested above. But it may be seen even more strikingly in the crisis which followed shortly after her entry into the novitiate of the convent of the Order of Carmel, Our Lady of the Incarnation, at Ávila. At that time she was twenty-one years old.

She entered into her new life with great zeal. She meditated upon the fact that she was very wicked and that, if she had died, her salvation would have been uncertain. Teresa's sisters complained that she was always weeping for her sins. At the same time she took delight in her religious duties and sought to mortify herself. One of the sisters died a terrible and painful death. The other nuns were afraid of this suffering, but Teresa had "only great envy of her patience." And so Teresa begged God that she might have to suffer an illness, so that she might win patience and eternal blessings.[7]

Her desire was granted. This scrupulous, fearful, and self-condemning woman began to suffer from "fainting fits" and "heart trouble." [8] So bad did her condition become that Teresa's father was given permission to remove her from the convent to seek a cure. As Teresa reports it, the treatment almost killed her— . . . "the pain in my heart, which I had gone there to get treated, was much worse; sometimes I felt as if sharp teeth had hold of me, and so severe was the pain they caused that it was feared that I was going mad." [9]

Teresa remained in this critical condition for about three months. She was sustained, according to her report, only by the fact that she had begun a life of prayer; and during these trials all her thoughts were of God.[10] Finally, one

evening in August, Teresa, after having asked to go to confession and having been refused because of her condition,
fell into a kind of a cataleptic fit. She was unconscious for
four days and was thought to be dead. Her sister nuns had
placed wax on her eyelids and had had her grave dug.

But it pleased the Lord that I should return to consciousness.
I wished at once to go to confession. I communicated with
many tears. . . .[11]

These episodes serve to typify Teresa's anxiety over guilt.
One could find other examples of this type of anxiety from
various periods of her life, but I must hasten on. Nevertheless, it will be helpful later if we take note now of
several other aspects of this anxiety over guilt.

First, it will be well to remember the physical signs
of anxiety in Teresa, particularly the heart trouble and fainting fits. Later in her life, when Teresa's more characteristic
anxiety is that of desire, her moments of deep anxiety are
often accompanied with these same, or very similar, symptoms.

Second, I should like to guard against the error of supposing that this anxiety over guilt can be understood solely
in terms of the negative characteristics of neurotic self-
condemnation. Relying upon Teresa's own account, these
black states of mind must be seen in connection with the
awakening in her life of positive love for God. Her old
childhood fascination with eternity is still with her.[12] But
more important, Teresa was beginning, just at the time
of the crises described above, to develop her life of prayer
and to receive mystical "favors." Frequently she was fa-
vored with the "Prayer of Quiet" and occasionally with the
"Prayer of Union." [13] As Teresa explains elsewhere, in the
Prayer of Quiet one is filled with profound joy and all one's
desire is to enjoy God.[14]. Or again, it is as if God has implanted a spark in the soul which grows to be a fire of

love for God.[15] In the Prayer of Union (with which, incidentally, fainting spells and heart pains are often associated for Teresa), we find, among other things, that most "intense and anxious desire for God," which will be discussed below.

Anxiety over guilt must be seen in the context of this positive desire for God. Even here, in what might seem at first to be merely a negative and self-concerned fear of the threat of Hell, anxiety exhibits its dialectical polarity. Fear of Hell, yes. But, also, sorrow at having offended Him who is loved. The consciousness of sin is expressed as *anxiety* because of and in the context of a desire for a positive good, the attainment of which seems threatened by the sin.

EMPTINESS

I might mention briefly another state suffered by Teresa for many years, a state which seems to have certain affinities with anxiety. This is a kind of "aridity" which she experienced for twenty years after the intense conflict which we have just examined. In one sense, Teresa's anxieties during this twenty-year period were not very severe. She became adjusted to convent life, which, according to her account, was rather relaxed. She regularly received visitors and gossip from the outside world. As a mark of respect for her family, Teresa was addressed as "Doña." Apparently she took comfort in this routine. Or, rather, she was inclined to take comfort, but this inclination came into conflict with other desires. Even though Teresa had given up any active discipline of "mental prayer," her mystical experiences continued. On one occasion Christ appeared to her and told her that her idle worldliness displeased Him.[16]

Toward the end of the period, Teresa's discomfort in her condition began to mount to a genuine anxiety state. It is, however, not an anxiety of sharp agony but rather one of disorientation, characterized by a sense of emptiness, or meaninglessness, or living with a "shadow of death" (see below).

On the one hand God was calling me. On the other I was following the world. All the things of God gave me great pleasure, yet I was tied and bound to those of the world. It seemed to me as if I wanted to reconcile two contradictory things, so completely opposed to one another—the life of the spirit, and the pleasures and joys and pastimes of the senses.[17]

Still speaking of the same period, Teresa says:

I can testify that this is one of the most grievous kinds of life which I think can be imagined, for I had neither joy in God nor any pleasure in the world. When I was in the midst of worldly pleasures, I was distressed by the remembrance of what I owed God; when I was with God, I grew restless because of worldly affections.[18]

The emptiness of Teresa's life was not mere emptiness. It was explosive, because she had moments of awareness of her condition and of longing for something more positive. In these moments of reflection the polarity of her feeling is quite clear.

I used to beseech the Lord to help me. . . . I wanted to live, for I knew quite well that I was not living at all but battling with a shadow of death.[19]

"Not living at all"—and yet alive enough to be "battling with a shadow of death"! At last the divided state could be tolerated no more. Entering a prayer room one day, Teresa beheld a statue of the wounded Christ (which, of course, she had often seen before). Such an impression did it make that she threw herself down before it, wept bitterly, and vowed that she would not rise again until Christ gave her the grace to keep forever from offending Him.[20] This experience is often called her second conversion. It occurred in her forty-first or forty-second year, a fact which is very impressive to those interested in explaining Teresa from a psychological point of view.

We may note in passing that the "vow of perfection" which Teresa made was followed by the most remarkable changes in her life. Almost at once she entered into a life of astonishing activity in behalf of religious reform. Furthermore, her inner life was transformed, so that morbid preoccupations increasingly were supplanted by an intense positive desire for God. In short, Teresa became the active, practical, indomitable saint who "moved the world."

Objective Anxiety

In terms of her inner development we are ready to turn to a consideration of the last and distinctive mode of anxiety. But it may be well first to pause for a moment to characterize a kind of anxiety that was thrust upon Teresa at this juncture by her environment. After her vow of perfection, Teresa began her work as a reformer of the Order of Carmel. This roused great antagonism to her within the order and, indeed, within the Church as a whole. At the same time, Teresa experienced a great increase in mystical phenomena. Her life was bent upon Christian perfection, and her new progress in the religious life was accompanied by mystical favors—visions, auditions, seizures of various kinds. This roused suspicion as well as antagonism. In the Spain of this period there were many cults of "beata," ultraspiritual women, whose orthodoxy was questionable, and often questioned. They were one of the prime targets of the newly rejuvenated Inquisition, and quite a number of these women were imprisoned, excommunicated, and even tortured by it.

It was not long before Teresa came under suspicion. Some of her friends warned her that she was being deceived by the devil; others, not so friendly, threatened to denounce her to the Inquisition. For several years Teresa fought this battle. Was she, indeed, deluded? At times it seemed plausible to her. Was she to end her life cast out of the Church which was everything to her? This seemed not too remote a possibility.

In the midst of these trials she found comfort for a time in the understanding and encouragement given her by a Jesuit confessor. The confessor, however, suggested that Teresa was not far enough advanced in penance to be able to benefit from her mystical experiences. Teresa responded by plunging into a frenzy of severe self-mortification: ". . . it seemed as though I were trying to take vengeance upon myself." [21]

During this period of "objective anxiety," many of Teresa's old symptoms returned.

> I was unable to pray or read, but was like a person stunned by all this tribulation and fear that the devil might be deceiving me, and quite upset and worn out, with not the least idea what to do. I have sometimes—often indeed—found myself in this kind of affliction, but never, I think, have I been in such straits as I was then. I was like this for four or five hours, and neither in Heaven nor on earth was there any comfort for me: the Lord permitted my fears of a thousand perils to cause me great suffering.[22]
>
> I was extremely fearful, as I have said, and my heart trouble made things worse, with the result that I seldom dared to remain alone in a room by day.[23]

After some months, and perhaps as long as a year, she found relief from this threat and the corresponding anxiety. Even during the period of deepest trial, she sometimes found comfort as a result of a mystical experience.

> When I was in this terrible state of exhaustion . . . these words alone were sufficient to remove it and give me complete tranquility: "Be not afraid, daughter, for it is I and I will never forsake thee: fear not." . . . I found my soul transformed and I think I would have maintained against the whole world that this was the work of God.[25]

It was, however, the understanding and support of such accepted saints as Fray Peter of Alcántara [26] which finally caused Teresa's suspicion to abate.

From this time on, that is, from a time roughly only two years after her second conversion, the dominant type of anxiety in Teresa's life was one which must be described as an anxiety of desire. This is not to say that there were no moments in which earlier anxieties came to the fore. It is, however, to say that they were more and more crowded out of the center of her life by a more positive concern. Teresa herself admits that such anxieties as those over guilt, for example, remained with her all her days. But they are now only a dark reminder that the new positive focus of her life was a gift from God and not an achievement of her own holiness.

DESIRE FOR GOD

It remains to describe that anxiety which I believe to be most distinctively Teresian. This is definitely connected with the renewal of her religious life, with its growth in prayer and progress in the mystic way. As we have seen, her re-conversion took place in 1556 or 1557 and, as she reports, initiated steady progress in her religious life. It is quite clear that from the outset of this new life, Teresa interpreted it as a gradual dying to self-concern and growth in love for God. She reports that her first rapture came to her when she was trying to decide, once for all, to cut herself off from certain ties which still bound her to the world. To aid her in this problem she was reciting the *Veni, Creator* hymn.

While I was reciting it, there came to me a transport so sudden that it almost carried me away: I could make no mistake about this, so clear was it. This was the first time the Lord had granted me the favour of any kind of rapture. I heard these words: "I will have thee converse now, not with men, but with angels." This simply amazed me, for my soul was greatly moved and the words were spoken to me in the depths of the spirit. For this reason they made me afraid, though on the other hand they brought me a great deal of comfort. . . .[27]

This took place in the year 1558.

Between the time of this rapture and 1560, by which time her "transverberation" had certainly occurred, Teresa was initiated into those "impulses" of love which are the most remarkable expression of her anxious desire. At last she burned with that "higher anxiety" (as it was called by St. John of the Cross) which, though it did not completely drive out more morbid anxieties, came to dominate her life and give it its impetus toward fulfillment in God. Though Teresa does not herself use the term higher anxiety, her thought on this point corresponds exactly with that of St. John of the Cross. In her *Interior Castle* she speaks of how true fear of God drives out lesser fears; how all of the many anxieties which arise in ordinary life are conquered by the single anxiety to serve God.[28]

The impulses of love to which we have referred are described by Teresa in various ways and sometimes under slightly different classifications.

. . . His Majesty began to give me clearer signs of His presence, as He had promised me to do. There grew within me so strong a love of God that I did not know what was inspiring me with it, for it was entirely supernatural and I made no efforts to obtain it. I found myself dying with the desire to see God and I knew no way of seeking that life save through death. This love came to me in vehement impulses. . . . Thou didst hide Thyself from me, and out of Thy love didst oppress me with a death so delectable that my soul's desire was never to escape from it.[29]

In her *Spiritual Relations* Teresa produced an account of the various kinds of phenomena which she experienced in prayer. She speaks there about these impulses of love in such a clear and concise way that I wish to quote her at considerable length.

Impulse is the name I give to a desire which sometimes comes to the soul without (as is most usually the case) having been preceded by prayer. It is generally caused by a soul's suddenly remembering its absence from God. . . . Sometimes this remembrance is so powerful and so strong that the soul seems in a single moment to have gone out of its mind . . . the soul's distress arises from a cause for which it knows it would be well worth dying. The fact is that whatever the soul then understands only increases its distress and it is the Lord's pleasure that its whole being shall get no benefit out of anything, nor remember that it is His will that it should live. It feels itself to be in a state of deep loneliness and total abandonment, such as cannot be described, for the world and all worldly things cause it distress, and no created thing can provide it with companionship; it seeks nothing but the Creator, yet sees that without dying it is impossible to have Him, and, as it must not kill itself, it is dying for death, in such a way that there really is a risk of its dying. It sees itself suspended between Heaven and earth and has no idea what to do. And from time to time God gives it knowledge of Himself, that it may see what it is losing, in a way so strange as to be indescribable. For there is nothing in the world—within my own experience, at least— to equal this: though it may last no more than half an hour, it leaves the limbs so disjointed and the bones so racked that the hands have not power enough to write: it also produces grievous pains.[30]

One immediately notices the striking similarity between this experience and certain of Teresa's earlier anxieties—similarities, that is, in terms of psychic content. Here again we meet the sense of loneliness, of having no way to turn, the feeling of being torn between Heaven and earth, the wracking of the body. Only the characteristic heart trouble seems to be absent. And we shall take note in a moment of other experi-

ences very closely related to these impulses in which the
heart trouble plays a prominent role. But in the experience
of impulse, the total context of the experience has changed.
The distress is related not to a feeling of sin or to an objective threat but to a desire for God accompanied by an awareness of one's distance from God.

In another place Teresa speaks of these same impulses.

. . . an arrow is driven into the very depths of the entrails,
and sometimes into the heart, so that the soul does not know
either what is the matter or what it desires. It knows quite
well that it desires God and that the arrow seems to have been
dipped in some drug which leads it to hate itself for the love
of this Lord so that it would gladly lose its life for Him. No
words will suffice to describe the way in which God wounds
the soul and the sore distress which He causes it, so that it
hardly knows what it is doing. Yet so delectable is this distress
that life holds no delight which can give greater satisfaction. As
I have said, the soul would gladly be dying of this ill.[31]

We have spoken of the transverberation of Teresa's heart.
This was an experience essentially similar to the impulses
described above, only the involvement of the heart in the
suffering stands out even more strikingly than in the example just quoted.

It pleased the Lord that I should sometimes see the following vision. I would see beside me, on my left hand, an
angel in bodily form. . . . He was not tall, but short, and
very beautiful, his face so aflame that he appeared to be one
of the highest types of angel who seem to be all afire. . . .
In his hands I saw a long golden spear and at the end of the
iron tip I seemed to see a point of fire. With this he seemed
to pierce my heart several times so that it penetrated to my
entrails. When he drew it out, I thought he was drawing them
out with it and he left me completely afire with a great love
for God. The pain was so sharp that it made me utter several
moans; and so excessive was the sweetness caused me by this

intense pain that one can never wish to lose it, nor will one's soul be content with anything less than God. It is not bodily pain, but spiritual, though the body has a share in it—indeed, a great share. So sweet are the colloquies of love which pass between the soul and God that if anyone thinks I am lying I beseech God, in His goodness, to give him the same experience.

During the days that this continued, I went about as if in a stupor. I had no wish to see or speak with anyone, but only to hug my pain, which caused me greater bliss than any that can come from the whole of creation.[32]

This sweet pain, this wound of love, is interpreted by Teresa to be the call of God to complete union with Himself.[33] It is an intense and burning desire which leaves her discontent with anything save Him. The desire is, however, an anxious desire, because she sees that she is separated from the object of her longing. The analogy, so far as the structure of the experience is concerned, with Freud's "unsatisfied longing" is striking.

In her *Interior Castle* Teresa further discusses this anxiety of desire in such a way that we are not only given a supplementary description but told quite clearly what the experience signified to her.

. . . [after receiving this experience] she is in a much worse state than before; for, although she may have been receiving these favours for many years, she is still sighing and weeping, and each of them causes her fresh pain. The reason for this is that, the more she learns about the greatness of her God, while finding herself so far from Him and unable to enjoy Him, the more her desire increases. For the more is revealed to her of how much this great God and Lord deserves to be loved, the more does her love for Him grow. And gradually, during these years, her desire increases, so that she comes to experience great distress. . . .

The soul, then, has these yearnings and tears and sighs, together with the strong impulses which have already been described. They all seem to arise from our love, and are accompanied by great emotion . . . they are like a smouldering fire. . . .[34]

As one draws ever closer to God, one becomes more overwhelmed by His goodness and, at the same time, more anxious to be united with this goodness. Therefore, one is also more anxious about any impediment. Such is the higher anxiety of Teresa. But it is still anxiety. She has not yet found rest or release; indeed, she still suffers the pains of anxiety which she had known earlier in life. Yet this anxiety is now, in a very real sense, creative. Under its urging she goes forward to a new integrity of life which expresses itself both in the progressive centering of her devotional life upon God and in remarkable achievements in the realm of active service. The anxiety of desire is not merely the outcome of this development. It is the inner motivation for the new life. As St. John of the Cross wrote, "If our spiritual nature were not on fire with other and nobler anxieties, we should never overcome our natural and sensible satisfactions. . . ." [35] In the presence of this anxiety one loses all fear of everything save that he might somehow fail to find fruition of the good which he has seen. One is delivered from manifold anxieties and becomes concentrated upon one profound anxiety.[36]

THE MEANING OF TERESA'S ANXIETIES

I have argued that before attempting a theological interpretation of experience, one ought to try to understand the meaning which it has to the one who has it. In the case of Teresa, she herself has written freely concerning the meaning of her anxieties. This self-understanding is revealed not only in her specifically autobiographical writings but also throughout her other works. Her most systematic treatment of mystical theology, *Interior Castle*, is very valuable for this purpose. To a large extent, her understanding of the matter has been given as we have gone along. It remains only to summarize.

I have singled out three modes of anxiety for comment, not counting what I called objective anxiety. I call these modes rather than varieties, because they are clearly interrelated in a complex and dynamic way for Teresa. The modes are anxiety over finitude and death, anxiety over sin, and anxiety to be united with God (anxiety of desire).

It is clear that, for Teresa, fear of death is related both to the anxiety over sin and the desire for God. Death is fearful because of sin and the punishment due to sin. Otherwise, death is not to be feared but desired, for it is necessary to pass from this life in order to enjoy full and permanent union with God. "I die because I do not die." Finitude is fraught with anxiety, but this anxiety is highly dialectical. It reflects both the possibilities of fulfillment and the dangers of separation. Even the more negative side of this awareness, fear of eternal punishment, has its full import only in the context of the desire for God; for eternal punishment means separation from the loved one. In her *Interior Castle*, where she is discussing the liability of all flesh to sin and the resultant threat of condemnation, she exclaims:

If that is indeed so, my God, let us die with Thee, as St. Thomas said, for life without Thee is nothing but death many times over and *constant dread at the possibility of losing Thee forever*.[37]

The dialectical quality of the second mode of anxiety, that over sin, is already implied in what has just been said. Anxiety over sin makes death dreadful. In St. Paul's phrase, "The sting of death is sin." On the other hand, sin is recognized as sin only in the context of an awareness of God. This awareness of God takes the form of a desire for God, but in the context of the consciousness of sin this desire also appears to be related to a sense of one's ingratitude to God, sorrow for having offended Him, and a fear of separation from Him who is desired.

If the anxiety of desire, the third mode, were not dialectically related to the other two modes, the desire would not be *anxious*. As we have seen, the desire is threatened by sin and death. Yet the awareness of sin and death by no means blots out this desire. On the contrary, where we are dealing with anxiety, the desire is presupposed. The sinner who agonizes over his sin does so because he sees and desires perfection. The finite one who agonizes over death is aware of the possibility of eternity.

The same dialectical understanding of anxiety would emerge if we could take the time for a study, in this connection, of Teresa's writings on mysticism. May I briefly indicate what emerges from such a study? The mystic way may be interpreted as a gradual shift from self-love to God-love. In Teresa's symbolism the soul must pass through various "mansions" before it comes to the center of the "castle." As the soul progresses, the attachment of the will is shifted from the bodily, to the spiritual, and finally to God Himself, who, in accordance with mystic doctrine, is to be found in the very center of the self. Whence comes the motivation for this shift? The mystic interprets this as the insistent call of God, who enamors the soul of His perfection. But this shift is not accomplished in a moment or without resistance. On the contrary, the natural inclination of the self to cling to sensual satisfactions and to the familiar world of material objects must be overcome at great cost. The call to abandon one's familiar world is frightening. The mystic way is "the way of fear."

The anxiety of Teresa, both as it presents itself in the phenomena of her life and as structured by the understanding of Spanish mysticism, would seem to suggest that anxiety may best be understood as the inner awareness which accompanies the agonizing movement from self-reliance to reliance upon God. Anxiety is fundamentally the child of love, for at each stage the dissatisfaction is awakened by an awareness, however dim, of a deeper good for the soul. Anxiety is the child of love, but it is a love which moves one through changes fearful to the fragile, finite self. This anxiety is a desire conscious of its possible nonfulfillment. Desire implies lack, loneliness, pathos; but more than this, it implies a positive impetus toward that which is lacking.

The same dialectic appears if one thinks of anxiety in terms of distance or separation from the loved object. Teresa speaks of being in "exile," distant from God. But anxiety implies not only distance but the *feeling* of one's distance. It is clear on the face of it, and certainly clear from the record of Teresa's anxiety, that one cannot *feel* distance or separateness except in relation to that from which one feels separated. Here we find the same polar phenomenon as appears in Luther's notion of the *Deus Absconditus*, the God who is hidden in His revelation and revealed in His hiddenness.[38]

Again the same dialectic is evident in the consciousness of sin. If one were simply and totally a sinner, how would it be possible to agonize over sin, to be anxiously aware of it? Anxiety over sin is the horror of the self at its own failure to be what it "knows" itself that it should be.

From the point of view of the individual who is anxious, one might say that anxiety is the personal awareness of the struggle to love what one ought to love, do what one ought to do, become what one ought to be. Anxiety is, so to speak, the inner side of the forward thrust of life. But for all of this, it remains an ambivalent, dialectical phenomenon. The thrust is painful; yet it is the condition of growth. The pain may arouse such fear that one turns his back upon growth, constricting oneself before the terrors of the unknown. But one may also live through the anxiety to find on the other side a deeper understanding of life. Anxiety is dreadful; but it is also literally a sign of life.

III

The Strange Work of God:
LUTHER'S INTERPRETATION OF ANXIETY

Je grőszer ein Christ, desto mehr Anfechtung.
LUTHER, TR 2, 1897 [1]
Nulla tentatio—omnis tentatio.
LUTHER, 3, 424, 10

From St. Teresa we learn that anxiety, apparently, is
rooted in a positive love or desire. Far from bespeaking man's
alienation from God, it signifies, even in its blackest moments, an underlying yearning for God. But has not the
argument been prejudiced by selecting a Roman Catholic
mystic? Both the tradition of Catholicism, with its stress
upon man's natural desire for God, and the tradition of
mysticism, with its notion of the inner divine spark, are
such as to foster the interpretation of anxiety which emerges
in the case of Teresa. Is such an interpretation warranted
by the experience itself? How would the matter seem when
seen through the mentality of one not biased by these particular traditions?

Martin Luther is the ideal test case.[2] I shall discuss
Luther more briefly than Teresa for several reasons. First, it
is not possible in his case to build up anything like a "case
study." [3] I shall rely, therefore, upon his statements about
anxiety. This does not mean that Luther knew about anxiety
only in a theoretical way. On the contrary, he insists that
he speaks entirely out of his personal experience (3, 549,

30). But with few exceptions the experiences are not related in a way that lends itself to biographical reconstruction. Second, the meaning of anxiety for Luther has already been discussed quite fully by others.[4]

Anfechtung AND ANXIETY

In his mature writing Luther preferred to use the term *tentatio* or the German *Anfechtung* (which is roughly equivalent) to designate the phenomena that interest us in this study. In the broadest sense, *Anfechtung* means any kind of "assault" which places one in spiritual danger.[5]

Luther's concept is clearly broader than the concept of anxiety. The assault may not take the form of anxiety at all, but may, on the contrary, consist in those tokens of good fortune which tempt one to pleasure, self-esteem, and a sense of peace and nobility (21, 103, 30). This comfortable frame of mind is even regarded by Luther as most dangerous of all. If we would understand him, we must introduce two distinctions at this point.

First, it must be noted that Luther sometimes uses *Anfechtung* to refer to an objective assault. I say objective because, according to Luther, all such assaults really come from Satan (5, 321, 15), who stands over against man as an objective enemy. Yet at other times Luther uses *Anfechtung* to refer to the terrible and anxious *awareness* of the assault.[6] Only this double usage gives sense to the famous dictum of Luther: "Keine Anfechtung zu haben ist die schlimmste Anfechtung! Nulla tentatio—omnis tentatio!" (3, 424, 10). The worst *Anfechtung* is to have no anxiety! One is in the greatest danger when he sees no danger. This is the cleverest wile of Satan, to make us feel that all is well, that our soul may take its ease. Thus, we may say that *Anfechtung* in the broadest sense is the assault upon the soul by Satan, the assault by which Satan seeks to rob us of faith. "Die Anfechtung will uns aus dem Glauben reiszen" (2, 691, 14).

But, again broadly speaking, Satan can use two quite different strategies: one is to make us proud and empty of the fear of God, and the other is to plunge us into despair (TR 3, 3108).

All that is experienced in connection with this second strategy, in which the individual is battered by despair, corresponds to the notion of anxiety as I am using it. It seems that Luther has come close to the understanding of many modern psychologists, who speak not only of states of anxiety but also of "anxiety equivalents," which I take to be ways of covering up the anxiety and making all seem well. But the "ease" and the anxiety are dynamically bound together; the ease hides the anxiety but also prevents one from coming to grips with its cause, and the anxiety prevents the ease from being natural or secure.

THE STRANGE WORK OF GOD

In many places Luther reaffirms his judgment that to have no anxiety is the worst *Anfechtung* (objective assault of Satan). This can be said in spite of the fact that, for Luther, experienced anxiety is dreadful almost beyond endurance. (I shall return to this theme in a moment.) For at least, in anxiety, one is aware of his danger. Indeed, it is Luther's considered judgment that anxiety is "the strange work of God" (3, 246, 19; 1, 112, 10; 1, 510, 24; 3, 246, 19; and 9, 101, 38). One could cite hundreds of passages to support this assertion. Let it suffice to point out that, according to Luther, anxiety is as necessary as food and drink (30, I, 17, 16); it is the birth pang necessary to bring forth life (11, 103, 15). How can this be so? Anxiety is the means by which God shatters our false security (3, 417, 10) and teaches us what true faith is (43, 467, 35). Anxiety is the school of God in which we learn to pray for faith (TR 4, 4991), or it is the oven in which man is tested but also purified (5, 183, 21).

Anxiety as Immediate Experience

Enough has been said already to indicate how contradictory Luther's concept appears to be on the surface. *Anfechtungen* are from Satan; but they are the works of God.
They are death; but they are the pangs of birth. This leads
to the second distinction I would like to make. At times
Luther speaks about anxiety as it is immediately experienced,
in the very moment in which it holds one in its sway. At
other times he speaks of it as it is understood in the perspective of faith. In the moment of anxiety it is dreadful;
indeed, it is death (10, I, 2, 105). One can scarcely breathe
and his heart seems to leave his body (TR 2, 1347). It is
as if a spear goes through the body (31, II, 248, 5). One
feels that God has abandoned him and that grace is suspended (42, 553, 29 and 40); one feels eternally lost, without hope (31, II, 110, 30); one feels that God is against
him (10, III, 149, 18). There is a "naked yearning for help
—without knowing whence it might come" (1, 558, 6). As
a part of this despair one feels a hatred of God, a profound
blasphemy (43, 654, 1). It does no good to rely upon one's
own experiences or presentiments of God; for God only
accuses. One can only flee from God (40, II, 330, 1). In
short, so far as one's own immediate experience is concerned,
anxiety is the mark of one's separation from and condemnation by God. So far as experience is concerned, what is there
to experience save one's sin? If there is any help, it must
come from beyond the circle of anything we know in this
dreadful experience. "Go out of yourself, away from yourself
to Christ" (TR 5, 5624). One can not receive the help of
Christ so long as he clings to anything of his own. "For the
bridegroom does not sleep with the bride when she is
clothed" (11, 43, 15). One must not count upon anything
which he himself has felt or experienced, but only upon
faith (40, II, 25, 4). As we shall see in a moment, anxiety
is a part of the divine pedagogy by which man is drawn to

true faith. But this is not a pedagogy which man understands, apart from grace; there is no curriculum which may be laid out and mastered from man's side. Indeed, so far as we can see on the basis of the experience itself, it is death and condemnation. Even though this is the work of God, it is truly a strange work. God remains hidden in it so far as we can tell under the impact of this experience itself.

ANXIETY FROM THE PERSPECTIVE OF FAITH

Yet this is but one side of the meaning of anxiety. This represents what is immediately felt. Luther, however, often speaks of anxiety as it seems to reflection, or, better, as it seems from the standpoint of the Christian believer. Bühler notes this same distinction and speaks of this latter viewpoint as "the knowledge of anxiety *a posteriori*." [7] Luther says these experiences are works of God which we do not understand *a priori* but which afterward are seen to be necessary to our salvation (44, 634, 14). Anxiety is the means by which God cures us of our self-sufficiency and brings us to trust in his grace. It is the loving embrace of God (44, 111, 32). But this judgment is from the point of view of faith, from the vantage point of one who has been granted the victory over anxiety (TR 1, 122).

IS A POSITIVE ELEMENT IMPLICIT IN ANXIETY?

The distinction between anxiety as immediately felt and as understood by faith suggests a radical discontinuity in the religious life. We might be tempted to conclude that, so far as the meaning of anxiety itself is concerned, man is simply separated from God. Now, in one sense this conclusion is certainly intended by Luther—in the sense that he insists that man cannot reason or feel or in any way find his own way from anxiety to faith. But I want to argue that neither logic nor Luther's actual descriptions of anxiety rule out the notion that an awareness of and desire for God are implicit in anxiety; that the quality of these experiences presupposes a positive relation to God. To say that man implicitly desires God is not necessarily to say that man can and will, because of this implicit desire, turn to God. In a similar way, a psychiatrist may find in a client a morbid state which, for example, could not be understood except insofar as a positive desire for the mother is predicated. (See the case of Hans, discussed by Freud, pp. 52-54 ff. below.) But this does not mean that the individual by his own resources can discover this or develop the positive desire in a healthy way. If this distinction is not borne in mind, all talk of man's desire for God will simply be labeled Pelagian in a doctrinaire way; and, I am convinced, an opportunity to understand the "image of God" in a fresh manner will be thereby lost.

One associates with Luther the doctrine of man's utter lostness apart from divine grace. It is, therefore, not surprising that he should emphasize that aspect of anxiety which is precisely the feeling of lostness. However, in a way which, I believe, does not at all weaken his evangelical position, elements of an implicit desire for God are presupposed by his treatment of anxiety, even the blackest moments of anxiety. If this is so, it would imply that, even in the sinner, there is not a total absence of that image in which man was created and by virtue of which his life was ordered to God, even if such a relic of our created goodness were held to be quite ineffectual in producing its implicit effect.

Take, for example, Luther's magnificent treatment of anxiety about death, which may suddenly be aroused in one who is "at ease" by "the rustling of a dry leaf" (1, 557, 11). The ease is swept away and the individual is gripped by the horror of death. As in medieval piety, Luther regarded death as the moment of greatest trial. At this moment Satan does his best to plunge us into despair, to make us doubt our faith, and to hate God. But the point which must not be forgotten is that, according to Luther, the anxiety of death is aroused by fear of Hell. One is anxious because of one's sins and the wrath of God (21, 111, 6). One fears rejection by the righteous God, who in the moment of death is very much remembered as the righteous one. "Oh, if I only had a sack of good works." If only I could live longer to pay for my sins (31, II, 248, 31). Because of this anxiety one seeks to flee from God, but the whole world is too narrow; one cannot escape from God (16, 418, 4). Indeed, Luther supposes that the heathen, *who do not know God*, may die peacefully. The anxiety is aroused only in those who know God (TR 2, 1944 and 3, 3140). In short, true anxiety over death presupposes an awareness of God and of God's righteousness; it presupposes a desire for eternal life with God.

Again, Luther says quite clearly that all *Anfechtungen* are assaults against faith (2, 691, 14). Faith must come first, but anxiety follows soon after (40, II, 29, 5). Furthermore, anxiety becomes more severe as faith grows. "The greater a Christian, the more anxiety" (TR 2, 1897). In the moment of anguish itself, faith may seem to be dead; but when the anguish is properly understood, it is seen to be a moment within the life of faith, namely, the moment in which faith is under assault. Sin and death would not seem so dreadful except against the background of a positive good which one dreads to lose.

Finally, it may be well to bear in mind Luther's personal struggle. In his years as a monk Luther was ridden with anxiety, primarily because of his guilt before the righteous God. He felt utterly lost, abandoned. Or at times he hated God because of His holy Law before which Luther felt himself condemned. Again and again Luther cried out: How can I get a merciful God? In this very cry one can see the dialectic of Luther's experience. Anxious over his sin, he nevertheless yearns for reconciliation with the One before whom he trembled. Fear of God?—yes, Luther knew what that meant. But this fear is really awe; that is, it consists not only in a shrinking away but also in an attraction toward.

Comparison with Teresa

Thus we find in Luther more stress than we found in Teresa upon the horror of separation from God which is a part of religious anxiety as immediately felt. This difference can be correlated with doctrinal differences between Roman Catholicism and Protestantism. Catholicism teaches that the image of God is not lost, though the likeness to God is. But what is not lost is a sufficient basis for a kind of natural virtue which reaches in the direction of God. The Reformers stressed the depravity of man, his utter lostness apart from grace. It even seems at times as if they are on the verge of declaring that the image of God was totally lost with sin.

These doctrinal differences are magnified by the practical polemics of contending historical movements. But I hope that our examination of this one area of experience, religious anxiety, will help to show that the doctrinal differences are mediated when we try to relate doctrine to concrete experience. For both Teresa and Luther were aware of the horror of separation from God; both have a direct acquaintance with religious anxiety; and both are finally forced to understand it as something which presupposes man's positive relation to God.

IV

Anxious Longing:

FREUD'S INTERPRETATION OF ANXIETY

THE RELEVANCE OF FREUD'S WORK

I stated in my introductory chapter that my argument would be developed "within the context of theology." Why, then, should a discussion of Sigmund Freud's concept of anxiety be included?

In Chapter VII I shall state why and how I believe an analysis of human experience to be of importance for theology. Here I shall simply assert that it is. Having taken this stand, it is impossible to confine one's attention to religious experience. For no sharp boundaries can be drawn between religious and secular experience. In connection with my particular topic, however, a more important consideration arises. Anxiety in the religious sense, anxiety "before God," is a *human* experience. Even if it is truly God before whom one is anxious, even if that anxiety is aroused by events and conditions not within man's control, it is still *man* who is anxious.

Earlier (Chapter I) I argued that Freud, as a psychologist, could speak of the psychodynamics of human experience but could not in this capacity judge the metaphysical status of the alleged objects of experience. Thus, he can help us understand the psychological dynamics and meaning of a fear of being bitten by a horse (see below); but the judgment that there is no basis in reality for this fear is not a psychological judgment. It is a metaphysical judgment, even though in this case it is simply made on a common-sense basis. The psychologist has every right to study the dynamics of a "fear of God" without imagining that psychology can tell us whether God exists.

With this distinction in mind, I wish to insist that there is no reason to suppose that the psychodynamics of religious experience display different laws than those exhibited in human experience generally. Indeed, if such were the case, man would cease being man when he is religious. Therefore, we should expect the dynamics of anxiety before God, so far as this is a human experience, to show the same structure as other kinds of anxiety. If this is so, I have a way of checking up on the validity of my analysis of the dynamics of religious anxiety. Do investigations in other fields show anxiety to have the same dynamics? If not, this would not *prove* my analysis wrong. The other investigations might have gone astray. But one's suspicions would be aroused. On the other hand, if my analysis is supported from other fields, this is one bit of confirming evidence—though, again, it would not of itself constitute proof. We might both, or all, be on the wrong track.

It is for these reasons that Freud's work on anxiety is of interest for my topic.[1]

THE SCOPE OF THIS CHAPTER

The above comments imply the scope and limits of my present concern with Freud. I am interested only in ascertaining his concept of the psychodynamics of anxiety. In the course of discussing that, I shall have to resist the temptation to wander into inviting side paths. For example, one could discuss the truth of Freud's attempt to "explain" religion psychologically, or his attempt to show that religious beliefs have psychosexual origins. These are matters of very great importance. But I must insist that they are irrelevant to my present inquiry. Even if, for example, Teresa suffered from a neurosis due to repressed sexuality, and even if her religious ideas reflect this psychological conflict, we are still faced by two independent questions: (1) What did her religious experiences mean to her? (2) Did her understanding reflect the true situation? The truth of beliefs is not determined by their origins or by their function in the psychic life of the individual—any more than the truth of Copernicus' hypothesis is to be judged on the basis of its (partial) origin in mystical, Pythagorean worship of the sun. While I would want to insist that Freud has shed much light on the psychological meaning of many religious ideas and practices, I will say without further argument that I have serious reservations about the notion that religious beliefs are caused by and explainable in terms of psychosexual factors alone. My point here, however, is simply that this important question need not be settled in order to get on with my inquiry.

Freud's Early Concept

Sigmund Freud's attention was directed early in his psychoanalytic work to the problem of anxiety, for he found that it was evidently related in a crucial way to the development of the neuroses. In some neuroses, like the phobias, anxiety was apparent on the surface. In others anxiety would often break out if there were any disturbance or failure of the symptoms.

In several places Freud suggests that there is a direct physiological source of anxiety. An "anxiety condition" is created whenever there is an increase of excitation without a corresponding means of discharging it. This notion of anxiety led Freud in his early work to take a deep interest in Otto Rank's concept of the birth trauma. Later Freud rejects the idea that the trauma of birth has any lasting psychological significance, for he recognizes that there is no evidence that the individual retains even a subconscious memory of this event.[2] Nevertheless, even in *The Problem*

of Anxiety, which came relatively late in his career, Freud
is willing to treat the trauma of birth as a "prototype" of
the anxiety situation.[3] The reason for this is that in the
process of birth there is just that increase of excitation which
characterizes the outbreak of anxiety. In an earlier book he
had said:

> To continue then: we believe we know what this early im-
> pression is which is reproduced as a repetition in the anxiety
> effect. We think it is the experience of birth—an experience
> which involves just such a concatenation of painful feelings
> . . . as to have become a prototype for all occasions on which
> life is endangered, ever after to be reproduced again as the
> dread or anxiety condition. The enormous increase of stimula-
> tion effected by the interruption of the renewal of the blood
> (the internal respiration) was the cause of the anxiety experi-
> ence at birth—the first anxiety was therefore toxically induced.[4]

Treating the birth trauma as a prototype does not imply,
for Freud, a recognition of this phenomenon as a significant
cause of anxiety in later life. But later anxieties have one
important thing in common with the trauma of birth: increased excitation which somehow does not find an outlet.
Though he later comes to see that this is not a sufficient
explanation, Freud holds on to this as a fundamental basis
of the anxiety situation: ". . . we shall believe that an increase of excitation underlies anxiety." [5]

Increase of excitation without a means of discharge may
also be looked at as a "danger situation." In his later work
Freud tended to stress anxiety as a "reaction to danger." But
this is not incompatible with those insights which were
based upon his physiological approach. Freud came to feel
that the physiological approach was not sufficiently penetrating. Still, it does not need to be repudiated but only "brought
into line" with later psychological insights.[6]

I want to underscore the importance of remembering
Freud's early physiological approach to anxiety. If this is

not done, it is possible, because of the later formula "re-action to danger," to think of anxiety exclusively as a shrink-ing, constrictive experience, forgetting that this negative reaction is linked with and cannot be understood apart from a positive, creative impulse.

UNSATISFIED LONGING

The indissoluble link between the positive and negative aspects of anxiety is exhibited nowhere more clearly than in Freud's review of the case study which had the greatest influence upon his thinking about this problem. The case is his "Analysis of a Phobia in a Five-Year-Old Boy." [7]

Hans, the five-year-old boy, had developed a phobia of horses. This became so serious that he refused to go out of the house, for fear of seeing a horse on the streets. He was afraid that a horse would bite him. Freud's conclusion, based upon a painstaking analysis given in the case study, is that Hans' real but repressed fear was a fear of castration at the hands of his father. This was feared as a retaliation by his father for Hans' "forbidden" love of his mother. Thus, we have the classic Oedipus situation. I do not wish to discuss all of the ramifications of the concept of the Oedipus situa-tion, but I want to direct our attention to Freud's under-standing of the underlying basis for the anxiety.

Hans woke up one morning in tears. Asked why he was crying, he said to his mother: "When I was asleep, I thought you were gone, and I had no mummy to coax with (caress)." [8]

Freud comments:

The disorder set in with thoughts which were *at the same time fearful and sentimental,* and then followed an anxiety dream on the subject of losing his mother and so not being able to coax with her any more. His affection for his mother must therefore have become enormously intensified. This was the fundamental phenomenon in his condition. . . . It was this increased affection for his mother which turned suddenly into anxiety. . . .

His morbid anxiety, then, corresponded to *repressed longing.* . . . He was with his mother, and yet he still suffered from anxiety, that is to say, from an *unsatisfied longing* for her.[9]

It is quite clear that Freud regards this longing as an essential element of anxiety.

. . . the beloved person would not withdraw his love, we should not be threatened with castration, if we did not cherish within ourselves certain feelings and desires. Thus it is these instinctual impulses which become the precondition of the external danger, its condition *sine qua non,* and thereby themselves a source of danger. . . .[10]

REPRESSION AND NEUROTIC ANXIETY

Why is Hans' longing unsatisfied, in spite of the continued presence and love of his mother? It is not enough to say that he is blocked from realizing his desire. This is true but too general; and, in this case, one can hardly see on the surface why there should be a blockage.

Freud distinguishes two types of case: one in which the impediment or danger is consciously known, and the other in which the individual has repressed his awareness of the danger. The former characterizes "true" or objective anxiety. It is entirely normal and constructive, helping us to anticipate real dangers. The latter characterizes neurotic anxiety. It is not constructive because it leaves the individual confused and helpless; for he is not aware of the true nature of his situation, nor of what really constitutes the danger.[11]

If Hans had remained aware not only that he desired to caress his mother but also that he feared his father's retaliation if he were to act upon his desire, his anxiety would have been objective. There would have been a better chance of understanding and dealing with it. As it happened in the case of Hans, however, he was unable to bear the awareness of this conflict between desire and fear. So the real desire and fear were repressed. Repression does not end the conflict but displaces it. The awareness of fear of his father, which he found too terrible to admit to consciousness, was replaced by a fear of horses. This, too, was terrible, but at least it seemed more acceptable to fear (and, in reaction, to hate) horses than to entertain such feelings toward his father. This is neurotic anxiety because it is not a preparation for the meeting of a real problem; rather, it hides the problem and makes it more insoluble.

ANXIETY AS A REACTION TO DANGER

In his earlier work Freud often spoke as if repression were the cause of anxiety, or at least as if it preceded anxiety. According to this view, repression removes the possibility of the attainment of the real object of desire and thus blocks the discharge of the psychic tension, which is then converted to anxiety.[12] This theory, however, left repression itself unexplained.

In 1926, Freud published his *Hemmung, Symtom und Angst* (translated as *The Problem of Anxiety*). In this work the whole problem is given a new orientation. An impulse can hardly pronounce judgment upon itself and, thereby, act as the cause of its own repression. Freud now argues that repression can be understood only as a reaction to some consciously perceived danger. An impulse comes to be regarded as a threat only because it brings the individual into contact with a real, external threat, or what is believed by him to be such a threat. In the case of Hans, to which Freud refers in this connection, the little boy desires to caress his mother. But this desire, he feels, will bring upon him the wrath and punishment of the father. Hans fears retaliation. Freud is quite clear that it does not matter whether any actual threat has been made or not, so long as the boy feels threatened. Feeling a threat from his father, the boy responds with a feeling of aggression toward him. The whole picture is further complicated by the fact that the boy also loves the father, insofar as this particular conflict is not concerned. Loving his father, he feels guilty for his hostility toward him. His relationship is ambivalent and exceedingly painful. The main point, however, is that Hans perceives what he regards as a real danger. How can the situation be resolved? He cannot flee from it. For, in the first place, he cannot just leave his parents. He cannot just renounce his desire. He cannot destroy his father, for his father is stronger and would in retaliation injure Hans. This is precisely the danger, since he cannot express his desire without courting retaliation. Furthermore, with half of his being, as it were, Hans does not want to destroy his father, and he feels that his impulse is evil. Not able to face what seems to be an insoluble problem, and afraid of being harmed, Hans represses his true feelings. In this case, the hostility toward the father and the fear of castration are repressed—and displaced upon the horse. It then becomes possible for Hans to avoid the anxiety by placing a restriction upon himself; that is, he must only avoid seeing horses.

Thus Freud came to believe that the awareness of danger precedes and provides the motivation for repression. This perception of and reaction to the danger is anxiety. It is a conscious state experienced by the *ego*.[13]

It is not the repression that creates the anxiety, but the anxiety is there first and creates the repression! But what sort of anxiety can it be? It can only be a fear of a threatening, external danger; that is to say, objective anxiety. It is true that the boy is afraid of the demands of his *libido*, in this case of his love for his mother; so this is really an instance of neurotic anxiety. But the being in love seems to him to be an internal danger, which he must avoid by renouncing his object, only because it involves an external danger situation. And in every case we have investigated, we have obtained the same result.[14]

The roots of all anxiety lie in the conscious awareness of danger.[15] On the other hand, however, anxiety is an expression of unsatisfied longing. How are these aspects of Freud's view to be related to one another? It must not be supposed that this is a simple matter; for Freud struggled with it all his life. Yet he does, I believe, provide a basis for a positive answer to this question. Freud feels that, in the developed state of anxiety, the inner longing and the external danger come to be dynamically related to one another. This can be seen in two ways: (1) through a consideration of the dynamics of symptom formation, and (2) through a consideration of his notion that the danger situation is always equivalent to the threat of the separation from the loved object.

Symptom Formation

Why are neurotic symptoms formed?

Since we have reduced the development of anxiety to a response to the situation of danger, we shall prefer to say that the symptoms are created in order to rescue the *ego* from the situation of danger.[16]

But why "symptoms"? Why not some other form of flight from the situation? The answer to this is very instructive and hinges upon the fact that the danger is intimately bound up with instinctual desires. One can flee from a wolf, or from a criminal. But in the case of neurotic anxiety one cannot flee from the danger in such a physical way, because the source of the danger is within.

. . . the beloved person would not withdraw his love, we should not be threatened with castration, if we did not cherish within ourselves certain feelings and desires. Thus it is these instinctual impulses which become the precondition of the external danger, its *condition sine qua non*, and thereby themselves a source of danger. . . .[17]

Since the internal desires are a source of danger, they must be renounced, repressed. But at the same time, they cannot simply be renounced, since they represent a fundamental aspect of the self, its very basic desires. Here the self is torn between fear and desire. The result is that some substitute way of expressing the desires is found. A symptom is nothing but a substitute for the expression of a desire which is regarded as forbidden or dangerous. Thus we can see that the process of symptom formation depends upon the double-sided, the polar, character of anxiety. Furthermore, in this connection we can understand why anxiety so often appears to be "objectless." The real object of desire and fear is repressed.

Separation from the Loved Object

Anxiety is a signal of a danger situation, which Freud defines as one in which the individual feels helpless, threatened.[18] Such concepts would certainly seem to suggest that the negative or morbid aspects of anxiety came to dominate Freud's thinking. This is even more clearly suggested, perhaps, by his statement that "one feels anxiety *lest* something occur." [19]

However, the essential polarity of anxiety is clearly implied in all Freud's work, even his latest work on the topic. For the danger situation is always identified with separation from the loved object. Here the polarity is clearly implied: there is *fear lest* something occur which might cut one off from the object of *desire*.

If we have thus far considered it [anxiety] as an effective signal of danger, it now appears to us, since it so frequently is a matter of the danger of castration, as the reaction to a loss, to a separation.[20]

Deprivation of this member [the genital] is tantamount to a second separation from the mother, and thus has again the significance (as in the case of birth) of being delivered over to the unpleasurable tension arising from the non-gratification of a need.[21]

Birth is the prototype of all later danger situations. And the anxiety affect which attends birth is the affect which is reproduced in all later experiences of anxiety. But birth is, literally, a separation from the mother. What constitutes the danger situation for the infant in the earliest years following birth? Freud cites the following: being left alone, being left in the dark, finding a strange person in the place of the mother. These "are all reducible to a single situation, that of feeling the loss of the loved (longed for) person." [22] The loved object ostensibly changes during the course of life, but it is always psychically an extension or sublimation of the love of the mother.

I should like to return in a moment to a discussion of the changing content of the loved object. At this point, however, we should notice that our discussion of the Freudian concept of anxiety has come full circle. We are back once more at the concept of unsatisfied longing, though, it is true, the implications of this "unsatisfied" have been unfolded in a fuller understanding of the terrible conflicts which give the longing the quality of "anxious" longing.

Anxiety is founded upon love, desire, longing. But the course of this love does not run smoothly. External, social obstacles (in the person of the father) confront the earliest infantile expressions of this love. The expression of love must change to a more mature and acceptable one. But the course of this change is full of conflict and fear. Nevertheless, the anxiety which accompanies the process never loses the mark of its original driving source in desire or love.

Later, in a theological context, I wish to suggest that the scholastic notion of man's natural "desire for God" is important in understanding religious anxiety. At that point we will profit from looking back at Freud's "unsatisfied

longing" for the loved object. While the scholastics understood and stressed the theological idea that man is ordered
to God as his supreme end, they tended to conceive of this
ordering (which they call "natural desire") after the analogy
of physical processes, such as the acorn naturally tending
to become an oak. The concept of natural desire is right,
but the analogy is wrong. A better analogy is precisely that
anxiety which Freud so richly illuminates. There is a drive
toward the loved object; but when this is understood in the
light of our experience of anxiety, it is easier to see why
the process should be as agonizing as men have always
found it to be.

Classical Protestantism has always suspected the scholastics of treating sin and separation from God lightly, and
the suspicion was awakened in part by such doctrines as
man's natural desire for God. However, if this doctrine is
seen in the light of the concept of anxious desire, the positive truth for which it stands may be embraced without the
suggestion that it minimizes the depth of sin and the need
for grace. Our image is not the image of the acorn matur-
ing, or of the stone falling to its "proper place." Our image
is that of the child with his burden of love, seeking gratification at first in a very self-centered way, finding himself
checked and bewildered in his first expressions, meeting
many dangers which threaten to frustrate his desire, losing his way, regressing to earlier and immature expressions,
experimenting with all kinds of substitutes for his first loved
object, needing the help and warm understanding of others
if he is ever to win his way through to a mature object
love.

FROM NARCISSISM TO OBJECT LOVE

In *The Problem of Anxiety* Freud states that as the individual matures, the content of anxiety changes.[23] As one
would expect, this is correlated with the fact that the loved
object also changes in the course of development. How

may this process of change be characterized? In the twenty-sixth lecture of *A General Introduction to Psychoanalysis*, Freud gives his answer to this question. He distinguishes between *ego-libido* and *object-libido*, that is, between love turned inward and love turned toward an object. *Libido* is the general term for the drive of the individual to seek the gratification of his impulses. Every individual does seek this gratification in one way or another, and in this sense we are all egoists.[24] During the early stages of psychic development the self not only seeks its own gratification, but *is* the object which gives gratification. In this stage the individual is not only an egoist but also an egotist. *Libido* is directed to the self rather than to external objects, and this is what constitutes narcissism.[25] During the course of normal development, the individual comes to direct his love outward to external objects. The fullest development of this tendency is what Freud calls object love. This does not imply that the self is no longer seeking gratification but only that the "other" is now regarded as indispensable to that gratification. More than this, the other can come so to dominate the consciousness that the self entirely loses its self-concern.

But when the condition of love is developed to its fullest intensity, altruism coincides with the investment of an object with *libido* . . . the sexual object becomes supreme; it has entirely swallowed up the *ego*.[26]

Not only other persons but also ideals may be invested with this object-*libido*. This is found in selfless devotion to a cause, or to God. Here, too, the self is lost, forgotten before the other, and yet at the same time it is fulfilled. The course of love runs, according to Freud, from early self-love to the mature love of an object in which self-concern may be overcome. To be sure, Freud thinks of this love primarily in sexual terms. Though for Freud the concept of sex was a very broad one, he is obviously far from saying the same thing that we have noticed in our analysis of religious anxiety. Nevertheless, so far as the dynamic structure of anxiety is concerned, there is a striking analogy between Freud and Teresa—or the Gospel notion that "He that loseth his life for my sake shall find it." In both cases, there is stress on development from self-love, and anxiety on behalf of the self, to love of the other, and anxious desire for union. In both cases the same paradoxical language is used. The self is swallowed up in the object; yet this love is the highest fulfillment of the self. In both cases anxiety is understood to be a phenomenon in which both fear for self and desire for the other contend.

CONGRUITY

I believe that it has been amply demonstrated that Freud's understanding of the dynamics of anxiety is congruous with the understanding of anxiety which emerged from our analysis of Teresa and Luther. At the risk of oversimplifying, one may say that if there were no desire, nothing would seem to be a threat; and if there were no threat, desire would not be anxious. Anxiety is a phenomenon of love or desire, but it witnesses to the fact that love is threatened from many sides.

V

The School of Anxiety

From no other quarter has the concept of anxiety received such lavish attention in our time as from the existentialists. Indeed, the experience as well as the concept is central to their understanding of the human situation. What is their testimony?

I shall concentrate upon the work of Martin Heidegger. Let me say that this does not imply that a discussion of Kierkegaard, Sartre, and others would not be fruitful. So far as the main problem is concerned, however, it would be largely repetitive. Sartre is more suggestive than Heidegger in analyzing the anxieties of everyday life, but his understanding of the concept as a whole is clearly dependent on Heidegger. It may seem more surprising to omit Kierkegaard, especially since his pioneer work clearly influenced all later existentialists, including Heidegger.[1] I do want to assert as strongly as possible that I am not leaving Kierkegaard aside because he would be embarrassing to my argument. On the contrary, it is, in a sense, too easy to claim him as an ally. I shall in a moment indicate briefly the basis on which I make this claim. Heidegger, on the other hand, seems at first to negate my notion that anxiety signifies a positive relationship to God—or to whatever is thought of as good and felt as desirable. In Heidegger we come closer to that understanding of anxiety which seems simply to say, "It is a sign of man's nothingness." This negative understanding, moreover, has found its reflection in modern theology. So, in Heidegger, we have a chance to test the value of this simply negative approach, to see how adequate this is even to the understanding of one who seems most sensitive to the dark and negative side of anxiety.

Søren Kierkegaard

The polarity of Kierkegaard's concept of anxiety cannot be missed. Anxiety is "a sympathetic antipathy and an antipathetic sympathy." [2] Or it is, in the words which Freud was to use later, an "anxious longing." [3] Anxiety is the reflection of man's ambiguous situation. As free spirit, "grounded transparently in God," [4] his life is open to infinite possibility. Man is called to be free, creative, open to the future, not bound by finite idols. As finite body, however, man finds infinite possibility dizzying and threatening. He feels the need of a definite arrangement of security. He is tempted to "grasp at finiteness." [5] Thus man both fears and desires his freedom, which is also his life in God. Ideally he could maintain this life "in faith," that is, if he trusted God for that security which his finitude demands. But in fact man succumbs to the temptation to find his security in finite things.

For Kierkegaard, then, anxiety points in two directions. It is the mark of our longing for God. But it is also the mark of our fear of God. When man, in sin, turns away from God, anxiety is not stilled. On the contrary, it is wakened in new forms. And in each form, [6] it points both to the futility of seeking to flee from God by this or that "grasping at finitude," and also to the fact that the desire to return to the creative, open, faithful life is still active. Thus, that anxiety which is a result of sin also expresses a dynamic dissatisfaction with the life of sin. For this reason Kierkegaard believes that the only cure for anxiety is anxiety. Anxiety is God's "school," weaning us away from sin.

Dread [anxiety] is the possibility of freedom. Only this dread is by the aid of faith absolutely educative, laying bare as it does all finite aims and discovering all their deceptions.[7]

. . . dread will eradicate what it has itself produced.[8]

Anxiety is the mark of man's creatureliness. But it signifies that he is a creature *before God*, on the one hand attracted to that fullness of life which is in God and, on the other hand, fearful of its demand of openness. Even in man's grasping at finiteness, however, his longing for God is not eradicated. It is this longing which makes him dissatisfied with, anxious over, the results of his attempt to flee from God.

I would not argue that, according to Kierkegaard, no man ever goes so far as to lose his longing for God. This is possible. But if he goes so far, he stands not in anxiety. Rather he is in despair which is "sickness unto death." [9] So long as one is anxious, there is a sign of life. One's way to God may be blocked, but the blockade is not accepted. It is assaulted. Anxiety and longing go together in anxious longing.

MARTIN HEIDEGGER

Martin Heidegger has given considerable attention to the meaning of anxiety. He regards it as a clue by means of which we may be able to understand Being.[10]

The aim of Heidegger's philosophy is a radical comprehension of Being.[11] This was the task which was set at the very beginning of western culture by the pre-Socratics. But the question of Being has never been rightly answered, because philosophers have always confused Being itself (*Sein*) with **one** or another existing thing (*Seindes*).[12] Metaphysics has failed because it has sought to demonstrate that this or that category (matter, mind, will), constitutive of a particular class of beings, constitutes the essence of Being itself. But this categorical approach can never settle the fundamental ontological question: Why are there any beings with any character at all? "Why is there any Being at all— why not far rather Nothing?" [13] The only answer lies in the primordial apprehension of Being. This apprehension is something instinctive to man, but it cannot be grasped by abstract thought.[14] The awareness of Being is man's birthright, but, as we shall see, this awareness is obscured by man's flight from Being. It is the task of fundamental ontology to recall man to his awareness of Being.

This basic orientation of Heidegger's thought toward the problem of Being is of the greatest importance for our analysis. In the first place, it means that every particular being, including man (*Dasein*),[15] is bounded by and ultimately determined by Being. Heidegger's view is not anthropomorphic. He explicitly repudiates Sartre's view that man is alone; that he must create truth for himself.[16] The nothingness which haunts man is not due to the fact that there is nothing transcending man but only to the fact that man has lost contact with reality. This means, in the second place, that the nothingness of man which is discovered in anxiety is not primarily a negative or empty nothingness; it is rather the surrogate of Being itself, positively "noughting" our feeble attempts to flee from Being.

The problem of Being cannot, however, be solved directly. For we are not Being; we are particular beings. We are finite beings whose view never comprehends even the totality of beings. Yet since Being is the ground of all that is, and since we are particular beings, we can gain access to Being in and through our own particular being. In the case of our own existence we have a privileged case: a point of contact with Being.[17] This is why for Heidegger the existentialistic analysis of man is a necessary prolegomenon to a theory of Being. There is no way in which we can abstract ourselves from our own condition of being in order to get an objective view of Being. The only way is through

an analysis of the structure of our own being which, it is
hoped, will expose its ontological ground.

Man is Being (*Sein*) under special conditions: he is
being-in-the-world. As we have seen, however, Being cannot
be defined. Neither can the special conditions, since they
are unique for each man. Man cannot be defined or grasped
by abstract thought.[18] The concept of "existence" in the
case of man points both to the concrete limitations under
which each man is determined and to his openness to the
future. Man is possibility within a context of given, unique
limitations. Since man is possibility, he is not finished and
is therefore indeterminate.[19]

Although man is indefinable, he has a structure which
is universal and which may therefore be characterized phil-
osophically.[20] Man means being-in-the-world. To be in the
world means to be a self over against not-self; it means to
encounter things and other persons. One of the creative
aspects of Heidegger's thought is his conception of being-
in-the-world. He rejects the Cartesian division according to
which there is a conscious subject over against a spatially
extended realm of objective things. Our world is not thus
constituted. "World" is not the sum total of natural objects (*Vorhandene*). This separation of a realm of neutral
objects is a late achievement of man which he values for
special purposes.

The original encountering of the world and the primary
meaning of being-in-the-world are in terms of "utensils"
(*Zuhandene*).[21] We find ourselves in the world as beings
concerned with our own being, and we know the other
beings around us first of all in terms of their place within
our concerns. The world therefore is a "project" (*Entwurf*)
of our concern for our own being.[22] It is not objectively
given to us, but is given to us as something which is ordered according to our practical concerns. Heidegger does
not mean to imply that this project is subjective or arbitrary. On the contrary, what concerns us is a function both

of the Being in which we participate and of the particular conditions of existence which are given to use.

Man is possibility.[23] Even though man is bounded by limiting conditions (this is his quality of "being thrown" into the world), he is able to choose what he will do in these conditions. It is because man is free in this sense that he is able to be and indeed must be concerned for himself. Or, conversely, it is because he is concerned for himself that he has possibilities.

Thus man finds himself in the world as that being in the midst of other beings who is concerned for his own being. On the basis of this analysis Heidegger concludes that the essence of man is "care" (*Sorge*). Care is characterized by Heidegger in the complex formula: "already being in the world, in advance of itself, as the being concerned with beings encountered in the world." [24] Man is a being who transcends himself. By this is meant simply that he is constantly moving beyond himself into the realm of future possibility. Man is a "centrifugal being" (*ein Wesen der Ferne*). "Man is always already beyond himself. . . ." [25]

Not only is man in the world in the sense of constituting a world through the projects of his concerns in the midst of utensils which he utilizes for his ends; he is also in the world in the sense of being-with-others who are in the world in the same sense. Man is a social being: he is being-in-common.[26] The character of man is constituted not only by his relations with tools and objects but by his relations to other human beings. Indeed, this is the most important realm: one's concern for himself as related to other humans is more crucial than his nonhuman relations.

As we have said, man is possibility. This means that he carves out his own mode of being through his concerns. This projection of himself, this construction, is, however, limited by the nature of things, and by one's unique situation. The root possibility, which determines all others in a fundamental way, is the possibility of choosing either one of two ways of existing. One way is the way of authentic existence (*Eigentlichkeit*), the other of inauthentic existence (*Uneigentlichkeit*).[27] Authentic existence is the free acceptance of one's being under the conditions in which it is given to one; it is keeping oneself open to his unique possibilities. Inauthentic existence is escape into automatic and anonymous living, seeking to avoid one's unique possibilities by conforming to what "everyone" does.

What does it mean to accept one's being under the conditions in which it is given to one? It means the acceptance of the responsibility to orient oneself in the world through one's own concern for himself. But this does not yet get to the heart of the matter. If this were the whole story, it would be difficult to understand why it is so common for men to be tempted away from their authentic existence into the realm of anonymity. There must be an aspect of man which we have thus far failed to mention, and this is the nothingness of man, which is apprehended in anxiety.

One basic aspect of man is what Heidegger calls *Befindlichkeit*.[28] This may be rendered as "the sense of one's finitude." It is the basic root of one's affective life. It refers, first of all, to the fact that one is "thrown" into existence under particular contingent circumstances, for no apparent reason. One did not choose the manifold conditions which limit him—his race, his constitution, historical period, nation, family, and the like. Yet, at the same time, one is not completely determined. This means that one has the possibility of choosing freely to accept what one is, and of doing with it what one can. One is called upon to express his being and its potentialities even under these limitations. This *Befindlichkeit* means that one is placed under a heavy burden and a challenge. One must continually realize himself under conditions which are strange, where there are no landmarks. Every achievement of the authentic self is a breaking of new ground. For the manifold conditions of each man are unique, uncharted. To accept this sense of one's finitude, to face the challenge of realizing one's unique potentialities in the face of this "dereliction" in the world, this is authentic existence.

But to exist in the world alone with no charted path is dreadful. It arouses anxiety. Anxiety over what? Over nothing. That is, no specific object awakens anxiety. One is anxious about being-in-the-world as such.[29] One is anxious because of the need to take responsibility for one's own realization in a world where there is no guidance. Unable to face this anxiety, one flees into conformity. One renounces his unique possibilities and does what everyone does. Here he gains a feeling of security. But he is unable completely to suppress the claims of his authentic being, so this anxiety arises ever afresh as a specific call to return to his true being, a call which the inauthentic man must continually repress.[30]

Another aspect of man, implied in what has already been said, is his temporality (*Zeitlichkeit*). This means, in the first place, that man is always in process of becoming. He is possibility rather than a finished product. At every moment he is making himself by his choices, and at no moment is his being ever finished. But the temporality of man means also that he is determined to death. In death his possibilities are extinguished, though still not achieved. Death reveals the contingency of man. It reveals his nothingness. Not only is one contingent because thrown into existence but because thrown there to die. This possibility of death, which is inevitable for every man, is the ultimate possibility, revealing the significance of every other possibility. And the significance which it reveals is—nothing! Everything is contingent, devalued, ultimately nothing. However, if one accepts this fact about himself and anticipates it, he expresses his true mode of being as a free decision. He exists authentically. He affirms the being which is his, even though he knows it has been given him under such annihilating conditions. When one accepts his ultimate nothingness, he does not therefore reject the world. He accepts it for what it is worth: a temporal arena for the expression of himself, but ultimately nothing.[31]

The nothingness of death also arouses anxiety. In the face of this anxiety one is tempted to try to forget death by becoming preoccupied with everyday life.[32] But, here again, the radical contingency of our being, which is the authentic way in which we participate in Being, cannot be totally suppressed. One's anxiety over death rises ever anew. It is both the dread of the conditions under which Being has been given to us and a reminder of our true being, a call to return and accept our authentic existence.

Anxiety is thus seen to be a radically ambiguous phenomenon. It characterizes man torn betwen authentic and inauthentic existence. It signifies the fact that man's authentic existence is contingent, threatened, and ultimately nothing. Yet at the same time it signifies that precisely this passing, slipping-away existence *is* what must be accepted if man is to participate in true Being. Let us turn now directly to the section in which Heidegger expounds his concept of anxiety.

If one were to ask Heidegger how he knows that authentic existence has the characteristics which he ascribes to it, he could not answer that this is empirically discoverable. Indeed, an empirical survey of human existence would be far more likely to uncover only inauthentic existence. For the life of conformity is "the average" (*durchschnittliche Alltäglichkeit*). Men as a rule do not freely accept their finite freedom determined to nothingness. They attempt to flee from it into anonymous security. How, then, it may be asked, can we know that there is an authentic mode of being behind this usual mask of conformity? We can know this because man can never feel comfortable in his attempt to escape. The authentic existence which he has denied has its revenge, or offers its call for a return, in the anxiety which marks every attempt to flee. Man's average existence has the marks of anxiety. This anxiety tells us that man is in flight from something. It is in the analysis of the flight that we come to know what authentic existence really is. Thus anxiety, this ambiguous and elusive phenomenon, is a basic clue in the construction of ontology. Put in another way, man's true being is hidden and suppressed in the form in which we ordinarily know him. Man is fallen (*Verfallen*). How do we know this? Man is anxious, anxious both *lest* his true being break forth and anxious *because* it is suppressed. Anxiety when rightly understood, reveals man's true being.

It is true that in our fallen condition the authenticity of our being is hidden and repressed, but this hiddenness is only the privation of a disclosure, which makes itself known in the fact that man's flight is flight from himself. In the "whence" of the flight, man's true being shows itself.[33]

This flight from oneself is not to be understood as fear. "The alienation of the fallen condition is rather based upon anxiety, which first makes fear possible." [34]

What then is anxiety? Heidegger first relates it to and distinguishes it from fear. It is similar to fear in that both are a reaction to a threat, a reaction of flight. But fear is a reaction to a specific object which can be located. Anxiety has no specific object. As Heidegger says, its object is "nothing and nowhere." [35] Yet anxiety is a universal phenomenon. Heidegger concludes that the object of anxiety is being-in-the-world as such.[36] Anxiety is the primitive awareness of the fact that man is threatened in the world, that he is ultimately determined to nothingness; he senses that he is not at home (*die Unheimlichkeit des Daseins*).[37]

This, however, is only one side of anxiety. As Heidegger says, anxiety is not only anxiety about (*Angst vor*) but also anxiety for or on behalf of (*Angst um*).[38] In this aspect, one is anxious not about a particular mode of his being; he is anxious on behalf of his authentic possibilities of being.

"Anxiety casts one back upon that for which he is anxious, namely, his possibility of authentic existence." [39]

Man is caught betwixt and between. His authentic mode of existence involves eventual nothingness; this threat arouses anxiety and tempts one to flee into the world of everyday conformism. But the flight from authentic being is sensed as a deeper threat and arouses anxiety which calls man back to his true being.

It is evident that in this analysis of anxiety Heidegger is much indebted to Kierkegaard, a fact which he himself acknowledges in an indirect way.[40] Here in a new guise are the themes of the temptation to flee from the responsibilities of freedom, the Fall, the uneasiness, and the call to return. There is, however, one immense difference. For Kierkegaard, anxiety is before God; and though anxiety is the schoolmaster which may bring one back to God, this cannot be done without faith, without the acceptance of divine grace which is really offered. For Heidegger, anxiety is before our nothingness, and the return to true being is the return not to God but to the resolute acceptance of our nothingness. Is this the final word for Heidegger? Does anxiety really in the last analysis proclaim that man is absolutely alone in a world in which there is no ultimate meaning, in which everything ends in a blank nothingness? One is tempted to rest with this verdict and to see in Heidegger the precise opposite of our contention that anxiety fundamentally signifies man's positive relatedness to God. Heidegger's work "What Is Metaphysics?" would seem at first to justify this conclusion. For here he states that the essence of man consists in his "being projected into Nothing." [41]

One's suspicions of a nihilistic interpretation of Heidegger ought to be aroused, if in no other way, by the fact that, for him, "nothing" is an active power which can be experienced. "Nothing 'nihilates' of itself." [42] Heidegger does not, however, leave us to such inference but states explicitly that the nihilistic interpretation is a misinterpretation.[43] The confusion arises because people tend to think of Being in terms of things-that-are. This is partly a result of the scientific mode of explanation. Science thinks of what-is, but it can never discover Being itself. Being is not a quality of what-is. It is rather that "Other" beyond the totality of what-is by virtue of which there is anything at all. If one tries to think of Being as a thing-that-is or as the totality-of-things, then one cannot discover it; in this sense it is nothing. It is beyond anything that is; science and common sense think of being in terms of things-that-are, and therefore to our ordinary knowledge Being is lost, and beyond the totality of things-that-are we can only imagine nothing.

Yet this Nothing functions as Being. It would be premature to stop thinking at this point and adopt the facile explanation that Nothing is the merely nugatory, equating it with the non-existent (*das Wesenlose*). Instead of giving way to such precipitate and empty ingenuity and abandoning Nothing in all its mysterious multiplicity of meanings, we should rather equip ourselves and make ready for one thing only: to experience in Nothing the vastness of that which gives every being the warrant to be. That is Being itself. Without Being, whose unfathomable and unmanifest essence is vouchsafed us by Nothing in essential dread, everything that "is" would remain in Beinglessness (*Sein-losigkeit*).[44]

Man is a finite being among other beings. He has, however, the unique capacity, manifest in anxiety, to be aware of essential Being. Both the poet and the philosopher can come to know this. But man is not faithful to vision of true Being, for in the light of true Being his own finite being seems threatened. Man therefore seeks to orient himself in a world of things-that-are. When his thinking and acting become accustomed to living in this realm of things-that-are, true Being remains hidden. Or, worse, men try to erect into a god some thing which they conceive to be the highest being. But true Being is not a being among other beings. It is the *prius* of all beings. Therefore, to man's ordinary vision it seems nothing. Nevertheless, if one is sensitive to the meaning of his anxiety, he can be recalled to Being. His dread at his absence from Being is founded upon a certain manifestation of Being. "Only in the clear night of dread's Nothingness is Being as such revealed in all its original overtness: that it 'is' and is not Nothing." [45]

This has a curious resemblance to the mystics' "dark night." It betrays an underlying religiosity to Heidegger's thought. Man, by steadfastly taking upon himself the awareness of his own contingency, may become the shepherd of true Being; he may make within time a temple for true Being in which it comes to a consciousness of itself. That we are not mistaken in attributing this element to Heidegger's thought is evident in his relation to the poet Hölderlin, and even more specifically in his commentary upon Hölderlin's poem "Heimkunft: An die Verwandten."[46] God is not really "dead," as Nietzsche said. He is only absent. One can still sense his presence far above the shining peaks, but one cannot find the right word to call him down into the midst of one's life. In this situation, one's task is to stay close to the region of the absent God until he discloses himself.[47]

It would seem, then, that Heidegger, too, is in general agreement with our thesis. Anxiety is not a purely negative phenomenon. The nothing which it discovers to us is not a blank nothingness; it is at the same time the positive awareness of Being and of our possibility of authentic existence. It is a tension betwen our fearfulness and our desire. Nevertheless, I question whether the assertions of Heidegger as to the relatedness of man to true Being are not in the final analysis empty. Being remains without content. It is merely that which is beyond everything-which-is as its presupposition. To be sure, it is dimly felt, but is this dim feeling anything more than a rationalization on Heidegger's part of his memory of the time in which he himself was nurtured in Christian piety? I do not understand how one can speak of God as being totally absent, or of waiting for His return. If He is totally absent, how would one know that He is absent? If He is totally absent, how would one recognize Him when He returns? Perhaps Heidegger would answer that God is not "totally" absent. After all, he does speak of the primitive awareness of unfathomable, unmanifest Being. My difficulty is that I cannot conceive of an awareness which has no content, which is totally unfathomable and unmanifest. It would seem to me that the presupposition necessary to account for the "anxiety on behalf of one's authentic possibilities of being" is a positive relation to that which defines, with some positive content, the meaning of "authentic."

CONCLUSION

From a different angle the existentialists help us to appreciate something we had already noticed about anxiety. So long as our attention is drawn to the feeling or immediate awareness of anxiety, it appears dreadful, annihilating; it seems to tell us of our nothingness. But when we understand the meaning of anxiety in the total economy of human life, it signifies a struggle, a tension, an ambivalent situation; it is the sign both of the call to authentic existence, or to faith in God, and of the impediments faced by the finite creature in responding to this call.

VI

Conflicting Interpretations

Underlying the anxious reaction to a danger situation Freud finds an anxious longing for the loved one. Lurking within the anxious awareness of nothingness Heidegger finds a dim apprehension of Being. Anxiety over death or guilt for the religious man apparently bespeaks some apprehension of and desire for God. All who have tried to describe anxiety in detail seem to support the conclusion that anxiety is a highly polar or dialectical phenomenon. In anxiety we are gripped by an apparent threat of nothingness; but we agonize over this just because there is something which we very much desire and from which we seem to be cut off. To sum up in terms of the anxieties of the religious man: he cannot be anxious over separation from God who has no positive desire for God (or who is *totally* separated from God).

If such a description of anxiety is accurate, as I believe, it might seem to point at once to certain theological conclusions: namely, that sinful man is not totally depraved; that he retains an impulse, as St. Augustine expressed it, to seek "some kind of likeness of God"; [1] that the image of God in man remains active in urging man to return to God. I am inclined, as a matter of fact, to accept these conclusions. But in all fairness, it must be remembered that description and interpretation are two different things. In many fields of inquiry, the better interpretation is often quite different from what a naïve reading of surface appearances might suggest.

In terms of my particular inquiry, it must be remembered that the whole tradition of the Protestant reformers and their spiritual descendants is opposed to the conclusions which I have mentioned. Is this whole tradition to be ignored? Were these theologians just ignorant of the phenomena of anxiety and their significance? This is, indeed, far from the case, as our earlier discussion of Luther should have made plain.

How does it come about that the same human experiences receive two opposing interpretations? In the remainder of this work I want to suggest two things which bear upon this question, so far as the problem of anxiety and its interpretation is concerned. First, the opposing interpretations result, in large measure, from dogmatic considerations. Second, an attempt to relate dogma or doctrine more closely to concrete human experience may help to mediate between the opposing interpretations. The dogmatic divergencies appear to be absolute. But, faced with the data of actual human experience, each camp is forced into distinctions and qualifications which bring them closer to each other. After urging these considerations, I shall argue that the phenomena of anxiety suggest a way of thinking of the image of God and of man's desire for God which does justice to the real concern of the Catholic doctrine of man's natural desire for God while retaining the insights of the reformed tradition concerning the dangers of that doctrine. First, however, I want to describe very briefly the two main opposing interpretations of religious anxiety. Most of the writers who should be cited in working out this contrast have not written explicitly or at length about religious anxiety as such. The way in which they would treat the subject is, however, deducible from their doctrines of the image of God, the Fall of man, and sin. For what is involved is the claim that religious anxiety indicates an unsatisfied longing for God.

NATURAL DESIRE FOR GOD [2]

Both Aristotle and the Neo-platonists were influential in forming the conviction which prevails in Catholicism that all things tend toward God as their proper end; that there is a kind of universal and natural appetite or desire for God. The Aristotelian notion that all things tend toward their proper perfection yields the above conception as soon as we realize that God is the source of all perfections, or that things are perfect only by participation in His perfection. The Neoplatonic notion that all things tend to return to the One from which they emanate also yields this conception, though perhaps with a different "flavor," when we realize that God alone is the One, that He alone is Being, and that all other things exist only by participating in His Being.

St. Augustine at the beginning and St. Thomas near the end of the Middle Ages, the two giants who still dominate Catholic theology, each have doctrines of the natural desire for God. To be sure, the former was more influenced by Platonism and the latter by Aristotelianism, and therefore their conceptions differ in detail. But of the main issue there can be no doubt: man in his way, as well as all other things in theirs, tends toward God, desires God, as his natural end.

Did these theologians perhaps wish to ascribe this desire only to man in his original created perfection, before the Fall? Protestants have no inclination to claim St. Thomas as a mentor precisely because, in his case, this question has an unambiguous answer. St. Thomas did not so restrict the concept of natural desire. According to Thomas, man in the state of original righteousness (Adam before the Fall) not only possesses a natural aptitude for understanding and loving God but also actually or habitually knows and loves God.[3] The natural aptitude is constitutive of man's nature.

As such it characterizes all men,[4] and it is not lost by sin.[5] On the other hand, the actual knowledge and love of God, the "gift of original justice," is man's only by virtue of a supernatural gift of grace,[6] and this is lost by the Fall.[7] In discussing the effects of sin, Thomas distinguishes (1) the constitutive principles of nature itself, such as the powers of the soul; (2) the inclination to virtue, which man possesses naturally; and (3) the gift of original justice. The first is neither destroyed nor diminished by sin. The second is diminished by sin. And the third is totally lost.[8] The rational powers and the inclination to virtue remain intact, even if the latter is somewhat diminished. These faculties are most important for our problem. For by reason the natural man can know that God exists, and this arouses in him a desire to know God more fully. And man's will is naturally inclined to the good. In pursuing the good, man is implicitly desiring God.[9]

Thomas' treatise on grace [10] makes it perfectly plain that he had no notion of teaching that the desire for God can be fulfilled without grace. But the grace which is needed to fulfill man's destined end completes rather than reverses the tendency which is natural even to fallen man.

If every agent acts for the sake of a good, as was proved above, it follows further that the end of every being is a good.[11]

. . . all things are ordered to one good, as their end, and this is God.[12]

. . . things "naturally desire to be." . . . Now, all things get their being from the fact that they are made like unto God, Who is subsisting being itself, for all things exist merely as participants in existing being. Therefore, all things desire as their ultimate end to be made like unto God.[13]

Man's natural tendency toward God is exhibited in various ways, in his desire for knowledge, or for beatitude, or in his capacity for virtue. In each area the quest for perfection is natural to man, though its fulfillment requires supernatural grace.

St. Augustine's relation to a concept of the natural desire for God is made problematic by the apparently great shifts in his emphasis, if not in his basic thought, as he grew older. The Augustine who wrote before the Pelagian controversy, the Augustine who wrote *On the Happy Life, Concerning the Teacher,* and even *On the Trinity,* most certainly held a doctrine of natural desire for God. In fact, his concept was more radical than that of Aquinas, for Augustine felt that there could be a direct intuition of God of a kind which was denied by Thomas.

Fortunately, my purpose does not require the settlement of the difficult and weighty problems involved in this issue. For I am concerned only to illustrate two divergent theological positions. It should be noted, however, that Catholic and Protestant estimates of Augustine tend to diverge along just those lines which mark off the positions under discussion here. Catholic interpretation tends to insist that the emphases of the early Augustine are not vitiated by his later, largely polemic, writings.

In the prayer with which he begins his *Confession,* St. Augustine is moved to say, "Thou hast made us for Thyself, and our hearts are restless till they rest in Thee." [14] This famous passage is a fitting commentary not only upon his life but upon a number of central themes in his theology.

The restlessness of man and his desire for God are clearly related in Augustine's consideration of man's relation to happiness, or to goodness, or to truth. The argument of *On the Happy Life* is an illustration. Man naturally seeks happiness, for the idea of happiness is imprinted upon man's mind. But man's only true happiness is found in God. God, therefore, is implicitly sought in every desire for happiness.

On the Trinity is no doubt a more mature work. In it the same kind of dialectic which appears in the *On the*

Happy Life concerning happiness is used in Augustine's discussion of truth and of goodness. Man's mind naturally desires truth. It could not seek truth if there were no absolute truth, the idea of which is imprinted upon the mind. Yet the truth which man desires is not a human truth, for man is conscious that he does not fully possess it and that he must struggle for it. Therefore, the truth which man desires exists independently and more perfectly than its reflection or imprint in man's mind. This independent and perfect truth is God. Whether he is conscious of it or not, man desires God insofar as he desires truth.[15] Augustine also gives an argument of the same form to show that man desires "the good" and, in so doing, implicitly desires God.[16]

Why does man's mind tend toward truth and his will toward goodness? Because God is actually in the soul as the truth which illumines and the good which beatifies. The concept of God as the inward Truth is beautifully expressed in *Concerning the Teacher*, according to which Christ is our "interior teacher." In another place, Augustine develops the notion that the mind of man exhibits a kind of natural image of the Trinity. In its knowing, remembering, and willing, man's mind is participating in God.[17] This is the image of God which may be obscured or defaced by sin, but which may never be totally lost.

It is, of course, well known that the emphasis shifted away from these ideas in Augustine's later work. Especially under the impact of his struggle with the Pelagian movement, he came more and more to stress man's sin. In this context Augustine insists that man is unable to love God apart from special grace. How is this to be reconciled with the notion of a natural desire for God? Roman Catholic writers have maintained that the later developments do not involve a repudiation of the earlier. In *On the Trinity*, St. Augustine distinguishes between "knowing" and "considering." The soul always knows itself and, through the divine image, God; but it does not always, because of sin, con-

sider what it knows.[18] The soul always desires God, whether
or not it is aware of this. Even sinners strive in all their
devious ways after some kind of likeness to God.[19]

The later Augustine insists that the actual movement of
man toward God depends in every case upon the intervention of special divine grace. But what that grace enables
us to do and makes us conscious of desiring is something
deeply implanted in our true being and never expunged
by sin. Our desire for God is always present; but it fails
of its proper expression due to our forgetfulness. Yet even
behind our waywardness there shines through a "striving
after some kind of likeness to God."

The concept of a natural desire for God is brought out
also in Augustine's idea of the natural "weight" of the soul.
Each soul has a weight which pulls or inclines it constantly
toward its natural place. Augustine interprets this weight
as the "natural love" of the soul, which instinctively moves
the will. "My weight is my love; by it I am borne whither-
soever I am borne." [20] Augustine is even willing to say that
this internal love is, in some way, identified with God, for
God is love. He concludes that every being capable of love
is implicitly loving God.[21] Every soul naturally hungers for
God.[22] "Naturally" does not imply that all men consciously
seek God; this is a normative and not a descriptive term.
Augustine means that all men are so made that their proper
or healthy functioning carries them toward God. Every
deviation, every sin, is an injury to *nature*.[23] It is in this
connection alone that we can understand the prayer of
Augustine: "Thou hast formed us for Thyself, and our
hearts are restless until they find rest in Thee."

It would be a mistake to suppose that the notion of a
natural desire is confined to Catholic writers or to the
medieval period. A host of modern Protestant writers could
be cited who, though they use a different terminology, agree
with the substance of this position. Friedrich Schleiermacher, for example, may be briefly mentioned. He con-

ceives of the religious life generally, including the Christian faith, as depending upon the emergence of a "higher self-consciousness." This is the "consciousness of absolute dependence," which he contrasts with two other stages of consciousness: the confused animal consciousness in which the distinction between self and not-self has not yet arisen, and the sensible self-consciousness in which this antithesis is established. At the highest stage there is a relation "in the unity of the moment" of the sensible self-consciousness to the consciousness of absolute dependence.

. . . when the sensible self-consciousness has quite expelled the animal confusion, then there is disclosed a higher tendency over against the antithesis, and the expression of this tendency in the self-consciousness is the feeling of absolute dependence. . . . The tendency which we have described, *as an original and innate tendency of the human soul,* strives from the very beginning to break through into consciousness.[24]

Evil, or sin, is thought of by Schleiermacher as "an obstruction or arrest of the vitality of the higher self-consciousness." [25] But so far from excluding that original goodness of man which is chiefly reflected in his capacity for this higher self-consciousness, it actually presupposes it.

But we must not think this means a state in which it is quite impossible for the God-consciousness to be kindled. For if that were so, then, in the first place, the lack of a thing which lay outside of one's nature could not be felt to be an evil condition; and, in the second place, a re-creating in the strict sense would then be needed in order to make good this lack, and that is not included in the idea of redemption. The possibility, then, of kindling the God-consciousness remains in reserve even where the evil condition of that consciousness is painted in the darkest colours.[26]

Consciousness of sin, and this would include anxiety over sin, presupposes a positive tendency toward God as the background against which the awareness of sin as sin develops.

> . . . sin in general exists only insofar as there is a consciousness of it; and this again is always conditioned by a good which must have preceded it and must have been just a result of that original perfection. The "bad conscience" which we may have within us is there, for one thing, only because of our seeing the possibility of what is better. . . .[27]

I must now resolutely put aside the temptation to adumbrate this general point of view further. The sources for such an undertaking, varied in expression and mood and yet uttering the same conviction, are scattered throughout the entire history of Christian thought. Enough has been said, however, to illustrate one distinctive interpretation of the phenomena under consideration: that is, the interpretation which insists that there is a desire for God which is not only not expunged by sin but which is even exemplified in the consciousness of sin.

TOTAL DEPRAVITY

A far different interpretation of the phenomena of anxiety is possible from the point of view of the Protestant reformers and their spiritual descendants. To a considerable extent that interpretation must be inferred from what is said of man's sin and God's grace. Yet the conclusions which must be drawn are hardly doubtful.

First, I think it may be well to remind ourselves that the reformers had a definite reason for being opposed to the "natural desire" concept. They felt that it implied that man could of himself merit salvation. Of course, this suspicion was intensified by the way in which they saw the sacramental system operating. The more one praises the natural virtues of man, the less real need he can see for Christ's sacrifice. And this was the charge of Luther against the medieval church: that it substituted man's capacities for Christ's grace.

The scholastic statement that "the natural powers are unimpaired" is a horrible blasphemy. . . . If the natural powers are unimpaired, what need is there of Christ? If by nature man has good will; if he has true understanding to which, as they say, the will can naturally conform itself; what is it, then, that was lost in Paradise through sin and that had to be restored through the Son of God alone? [28]

The point at issue here is extremely important. Does a concept of natural desire imply that man may merit salvation without the grace of Christ? As I said above, Aquinas would certainly deny this. And it is now plain that Luther would affirm it. I wish to insist, however, that Luther is protesting against the doctrine as it had come, in his opinion, to be reflected in certain historical institutions. No doubt the possibilities of construing the concept in a Pelagian sense had been actualized by large segments of the medieval Church. But one can hardly read Aquinas without realizing that this line of development, which came to stress human merit, is not necessarily implied in the concept of natural desire and that such an interpretation was in fact not intended by Aquinas. Doctrinal differences are shaped and exaggerated by the exigencies of the struggle against certain historical institutions.

The Protestant position on this matter came to be expressed in a doctrine of "total depravity." It remains clear in the writings of Luther and Calvin that this point of view, which had not yet hardened into a separate doctrine, was maintained for one very simple religious reason: to guard the conviction that God in Christ takes the initiative in salvation. Later, however, the doctrine was elaborated and made rigid by means of metaphysical definitions and distinctions.

One side of the doctrine of total depravity is the notion

that all acts and desires of the natural man, since Adam's fall, are sinful and that they can in no wise tend towards God. Writes Luther:

Hence it is great wisdom to know that we are nothing but sin, so that we do not think of sin as lightly as do the pope's theologians, who define sin as "anything said, done, or thought against the Law of God." Define sin, rather, on the basis of this psalm, as all that is born of father and mother. . . . From such a root nothing good before God can come forth.[29]

Calvin explicitly denies "that men destitute of grace have some motions towards true goodness, though ever so feeble." [30] After presenting excerpts from many writers of the reformed tradition on this point, Heinrich Heppe sums up the matter in these dramatic words:

Man, dead in sin, is only passively related to the activity of the Holy Spirit in grace, and so far as he is self-active, can only resist it, *so that grace must literally break man's natural anti-God will*, in order to convert him to itself.[31]

This position is meant to deny that man, on his own, can even do anything to prepare for the coming of God's special grace.

Farewell, then, all the idle observations of many writers concerning "preparations"; for although the faithful sometimes petition that their hearts may be conformed to the Divine Law, yet it should be remarked that even this desire of praying originates from God.[32]

Man as such is totally bereft of any desire for the true God.

According to John Knox, through original sin "was the image of God utterly defaced in man; and he and his posterity became enemies to God, slaves to Satan, and servants to sin." [33] Further, in discussing the origin of faith, Knox says:

This our faith . . . proceeds not from flesh and blood, that is to say, from no natural powers within us, but is the inspiration of the Holy Ghost. . . . For of nature we are so dead, so blind and so perverse, that neither can we feel when we are pricked, see the light when it shines, nor assent to the will of God when it is revealed. . . . For of ourselves we are not sufficient to think one good thought. . . .[34]

It must not be supposed that this tradition is a thing of the past. It is very much alive in the so-called neo-Reformation theology of the Continent, for which Karl Barth must be regarded as chief spokesman.[35] This comes out in a way which is instructive for our theme in the very manner in which he arranges his dogmatic materials. In his *Church Dogmatics* the treatment of man's sinful condition follows his discussion of Christ's saving action. Is this not a reversal of the proper order? Barth is, of course, perfectly aware that the sinful condition preceded Christ's action in the order of history. But he wishes to call attention to a conviction which he regards as an essential part of the Christian faith: namely, that we can have no knowledge of sin as sin before we are redeemed by Christ. Where else, he asks, than in the light of Christ should we come to know about sin as sin? *To suppose a prior awareness of sin would be to suppose also a prior awareness of God!* Consciousness of sin and consciousness of God are correlative.[36]

Is this not just the conclusion which emerged from the study, for example, of Teresa? Yes—and no. It is true that there we arrived at the notion that anxiety over sin implies a positive awareness of God. But the perspective was entirely different. It was suggested that this implied a natural desire for God. For Barth there is a correlation of awareness of sin and awareness of God for just the opposite reason: namely, there can be no awareness of sin until after man has been reached and changed by God's grace in Christ. Then, of course, in the light of what God has done, the agony over our dereliction comes to us. Far from implying a "natural desire" for God, the situation implies that, apart

from grace, we are so dead in sin that we cannot even take
sin seriously as sin.[37] In Karl Barth, then, the "opposite"
interpretation of man's anxiety comes to clearest expression. One can even go farther and say that this human desire
for God, so far from being an expression of fallen man's
positive relation to the true God, is an expression of man's
futile attempt to divest himself of the true God and to
find a false but more comforting God.

In the place of obedience and faith, in which man could
live in peace with God, fallen man brings forth that frenzied
and unfruitful dialectic, so-called "religion," which is an attempt to lift one's own soul up to God. . . .[38]

Man's desire for God is a tragicomic surrogate for a relation
to the true God. To be sure, it gives perverted witness that,
even in sin, man is never out of relation to God. But the
relationship in this case is one of man's pride, his seeking to
fulfill himself through a relation to a "divinity" which is
of his own imagining, and of God's judgment upon this
idolatry.

In contrast, then, to the notion of a natural virtue which
points us Godward we have the notion of a depravity so
total that what seems to be a desire for God is really "un-
faith" [39] or a demonic desire which only hides from us the
fact that we do not know or desire the true God.

Thus far, however, I have commented only on Barth's
judgment of those states of mind which are to be ascribed
to fallen man. Yet I have already intimated that there is
another side to the coin: that once God's grace in Christ
has reached us, we can become aware of sin as sin. This
means to be aware of its horror, to be brought into a fruitful anxiety. As he makes plain in section 6, 3 in the first
volume of his *Dogmatics*, Barth has a place in his theology
for a discussion of human experiences. But he argues that
we must reverse the relation of theology to experience which
found expression in the work of Schleiermacher. We can-

not understand God or the Word of God by reflecting on experience. On the contrary, we can understand experience rightly only in the light of the Word of God.

Barth distinguishes between the true consciousness of sin, which rests upon a prior acknowledgement of the grace of Christ, and that self-judgment which might seem to some to be an independent consciousness of sin. So far as our natural self-understanding goes, we cannot be conscious of sin but only of inner tension, of limitations and frustrations, of a vague but painful sense of unfulfillment. We can become aware that we are a problem to ourselves but not that our problem is "sin before God." [40] On the other hand, the reception of grace through Christ does not eliminate our anxieties. Rather it sheds light upon them, so that we can see our wretchedness more clearly.

True anxiety [*Anfechtung*] arises not so much from the insecurities of historical existence but from the nature of the self-confidence of the man who has been justified by God, and for whom such insecurities and suspicions have already been broken and put behind. He really does have such a self-confidence. . . . But that simply means . . . that he has renounced all illusions that it is he himself who overcomes the dangers of his situation. . . . Now he knows that, so far as he himself is concerned, he has no advocate, and whatever he might bring forth as an advocate is struck from his hands.[41]

Furthermore, Barth says that we see in the incarnate Christ the picture of that human existence which he came to redeem. And here we see that man is a slave, a prisoner, despised and rejected, not only beset by insecurities but betrayed and defenseless.[42]

In commenting upon II Corinthians 7:8-11, Barth discusses the twofold nature of λυπη (which he translates as *Betrübnis*, affliction or sorrow). Though not quite the same concept as anxiety, this affliction is related to the twofold nature of anxiety, that of the sinner and that which stems from grace. Barth says that there is an affliction which comes from God and is a sorrow over the perversion of ourself which is seen in the light of God's disclosure. This kind of affliction, while it really has the character of an affliction, contains no hopeless remorse. It is in contrast to the affliction which comes from the world, which is full of remorse and leads to death. Barth rejects the notion that this worldly affliction can be regarded (or was regarded by Paul) "as a kind of preface" to the affliction which has its source in God.[43]

One does not find in Barth an extended and direct discussion of anxiety. Nevertheless, on the basis of what has been said, it is clear that he stands in the tradition of the Reformation on the doctrine of total depravity. And it is clear how the phenomena of anxiety must be treated, in general, from this point of view.

THE ALTERNATIVES

It is now possible to state briefly the problem of interpreting theologically the phenomena of anxiety. I have shown that people of various backgrounds give similar descriptions of anxiety, so far as its dynamics are concerned. But I have also shown how divergent theological interpretations of the data are given, and how these divergencies are related to dogmatic considerations.

On the one hand, it is possible to understand religious anxiety as a genuine desire for God, as expressing the upward thrust of that goodness of man which is not utterly lost by sin.

On the other hand, however, it is possible to see in the data a reflection of a human situation which is consistent with the notion of man's total depravity. It is true that the interpretation in this case is a bit more complex. For it is necessary to treat separately the anxiety of the sinner and the anxiety of the man redeemed by grace. There is no continuity between the two. The anxiety of the sinner is the expression of his tendency to erect false gods and to seek his security in them. The anxiety of the redeemed man is simply a fuller recognition of the horror and insecurity of ordinary human life, of the blackness of sin, and the like. It is a recognition that, so far as one's own strength and goodness go, one can still slip back into that Hell and nothingness. To be sure, this retrospective horror goes along with a profound gratitude to Christ, and this implies a kind of "desire for God." At least God is now seen as one's only good; but the redeemed man understands that his new positive relation to God depends not upon his desire but only upon God's grace. If any man does in any sense desire God, it is only because and insofar as he has received the redeeming grace of God. Desire for God may be admitted, but not as natural.

How are we to go forward from this point? Can we go forward? Must we just say that descriptions of human experiences are irrelevant to theology, since the descriptions apparently may be made to fit in with such contradictory theories? Must we admit that theology is dogmatically determined, that from an established dogmatic position we may characterize and explain our experience, but that we can admit no influence in the reverse direction?

Furthermore, even more serious questions arise for anyone who insists that there is an empirical element in all thought, including theology. It is a commonplace in contemporary philosophy to say that any hypothesis or theory which cannot, in principle, be tested by an appeal to experience is arbitrary and meaningless. Is this the situation of theology, that it is empirically arbitrary and meaningless? For apparently opposing doctrines of man seem to be reconcilable with the same descriptions of an area of human experience which, it seems, should be relevant to an understanding of man. Are the opposing doctrines equally good, or equally bad?

Finally, does experience have any role to play in answering these questions? How is experience related to theology?

VII

Theology and Experience

The experience of anxiety has a certain structure. Whether described by Catholic mystic, agnostic existentialist, or atheist psychoanalyst, it exhibits a specific character. That character is anxious longing. The experience itself is constituted by a polar tension between fear and longing. In some sense longing, or love, is fundamental. Anxiety is desire aware of a threat to its fulfillment.

This descriptive (phenomenological) approach to anxiety could be extended indefinitely. But the time has come to ask whether such an undertaking has any significance for theology—I mean for theology as the concern with the reality and nature of God and of His relation to man. After all, even if my characterization of anxiety is correct, it simply describes certain human states of awareness. Does the human feeling that one desires God tell us anything about an objectively real God—even that there is such a reality? Is not my whole inquiry of interest only to psychology (even if "psychology of religion") and not at all to theology? Does the inquiry into the nature of religious anxiety help at all in discriminating better from worse theology?

In certain realms of inquiry the relations between experience and interpretation seem to be well understood. The clearest models of this are found in the realm of the natural sciences. Explanatory concepts or theories are ways of designating a recurrent order of events. Whether one interprets science idealistically, and says that it seeks to designate the recurrent order of aspects of experience; or whether one interprets science realistically, and says that it seeks to designate the recurrent order of aspects of a transcendent "world"—in either case the evidence of the recurrent order is given in experience. Even the realist must speak of the order of experience as his evidence for the character of the world beyond experience.

The positivists or logical empiricists have clarified the implications of the reliance of the natural sciences upon the order of experience.[1] They have pointed out that both the meaning and the truth of a statement depend upon its relation to experience. That is, a statement is meaningful if and only if one can in principle designate certain kinds of experience which would (if they occurred) confirm or disconfirm the statement. And the statement is true if and only if those experiences would confirm the statement. Thus, the statement "There is a one-thousand-carat diamond at the center of the earth" is meaningful *because* one can designate certain conceivable (even if not actually forthcoming) experiences by which it could be confirmed or disconfirmed. And the statement is true or untrue *because* those experiences would confirm or disconfirm.

It is possible, as the positivists have demonstrated, to work out the logic of scientific explanation. When this is done, it is apparent that theory is closely tied to experience. That is, *it is because the order of our experience has one specific character and not another* that a particular theory or alleged explanation is regarded as better or worse than another.

Is anything like this true in the realm of theology? Does experience make any difference in determining what doctrines are true, or at least closer to the truth?

Two very powerful schools of thought, positivism and Barthianism, would say "No!" The positivists, and many so-called analytic philosophers, would say "No" on the

grounds that the doctrines of theology cannot in principle
be confirmed or disconfirmed by experience. This being so,
the question of the truth of these doctrines does not even
arise; for they are simply meaningless. They may, to be sure,
have an emotive or hortatory significance; but they are cog-
nitively meaningless. They tell us nothing about what does
or does not exist.

This general point of view, shared by positivists and some
linguistic analysts, has received a brilliant and classical statement in an article by John Wisdom entitled "Gods." [2] In
this article Wisdom examines the relation between our experience and the belief that a divine Mind ordered or de-
signed the universe. His contention is that the believer in
the divine, ordering Mind will allow no particular experience
to count against his belief; while the disbeliever will allow
no experience to count for it. If the disbeliever points to a
particular example of disorder, the believer replies that we
just don't see the whole picture, or that God's mind should
not be measured by ours, or the like. In this way, says Wisdom, the original contention (that a divine Mind orders
all things for good) dies a "death by a thousand qualifications." The point is that by arguing in this way the believer
has shown that his belief implies no *particular* state of af-
fairs which experience can either confirm or disconfirm. And
therefore the belief or doctrine tells us nothing about why
things should be this way rather than that; it is empty of
any definite implication for the order of our experience.

Does not the argument of Chapter VI support Wisdom's
general position? Did we not discover that the phenomena
of anxiety may be accounted for by two quite contradictory
theological doctrines? Perhaps both the doctrines of natural
desire and of total depravity are vacuous. Perhaps they could
be made compatible with any description of man's anxiety
and, therefore, not imply anything definite. Thus, if man
appears to have no glimmer of a desire for God, this only

confirms his total depravity. If, on the other hand, he does seem to desire God, this again only shows his depravity— for he does not *really* desire *God;* he really desires the fulfillment of his own selfish wishes which he has projected as an idea of God.

Thus contemporary philosophical empiricism tends to be critical of theology because, it feels, theology is insensitive to the structure of actual, human experience. The accusation is that theology imposes a structure upon experience and does not seek to verify its concepts by experience.

Karl Barth and his followers would agree that experience is of no value in determining what theological doctrines are true. But Barth would draw from this quite a different conclusion than the empiricists: not that this makes theology vacuous, but that true theology has a basis which utterly transcends the structures of human experience, namely, the Word of God.

The position of Karl Barth is so influential and, in its own right, so important that I wish to deal with it at some length. In fact, Barth's rejection of experience as a criterion of theological doctrine is involved with many other issues pertinent to my inquiry. Therefore, I shall make my extended comments on Barth in a separate chapter (VIII).

Before turning to my own answer to the question "Does experience have any relevance for theology?" I should like simply to note that there are two important schools of thought which would reply "Yes." I refer to Thomism and to modern so-called empirical theology. Both hold that rational reflection upon experience can give knowledge of God, though in other respects these theologies are widely divergent.

There is a sense in which these schools are, in my opinion, too dependent upon the view that theological truths may be derived inductively. That is, they seem to feel that *the* meaning of experience can be, as it were, read off from ex-

perience itself. In the case of Thomism, this view goes along
with the Aristotelian confidence in the process of rational
induction. In the case of an empiricist like H. N. Wieman
it is accompanied by a certain view of the methods of modern science, which he takes as a model for theology. In
both cases the "free play" which can and does characterize
the processes of rational construction is unduly minimized.

I should like to dwell upon this element of free play for
a moment, for it affects my own view of the relation between theology and experience.

There are two ways in which free play may be empha-
sized. One, which I do not personally find too congenial,
is the way of philosophical idealism. When applied to the
interpretation of scientific method, such idealism suggests
that scientific concepts or laws are not (as it were) more or
less adequate pictures of a transcendent reality but are con-
structs more or less freely devised by reason (or imagination) to bring coherence into the mass of events-as-experi-
enced. Thus our concepts are not determined by an outside,
objective or neutral world. The world is, on the contrary,
simply a name for the system of concepts which we choose,
with considerable freedom, to impose upon our experience.
The mind is active and creative in determining the categories of reality.

It is quite possible to interpret science idealistically, as,
for example, Eddington has done. The idealistic tendency
is suggested in some, though by no means all, of the writings
of Einstein—by his statement, for example, that "Science is
not just a collection of laws, a catalogue of unrelated facts.
It is a creation of the human mind, with its freely invented
ideas and concepts." [3]

There is another and more cautious way of stressing the
element of free play in the process of arriving at scientific
concepts or laws. I have in mind a group of thinkers, of
whom we may regard C. Hempel as typical, who want to

remain realistic in their philosophy. While acknowledging the creative role of the mind in the process of theory formation, they deny that this implies an inability of science to come progressively closer to objective knowledge of the world which transcends our experiences and concepts. But I do not wish to launch a discussion of the details of the idealist-realist controversy. Both agree that, even in the so-called exact sciences, the data (experience) do not uniquely determine one true explanatory hypothesis. There is a "leap to the hypothesis" in which imagination undoubtedly plays a large role.

What I am trying to say may be illustrated by the much-discussed situation in theories concerning the nature and behavior of light. Modern physics has at its disposal a great deal of rather precise data concerning light. But shall light be considered as a wave or as a particle phenomenon? Wave theories and particle theories are quite different. Common sense says that light cannot be both. Each theory seems to cover part of the data better than its rival. Now, of course, the time may very well come when yet a third theory is developed which seems to be adequate to all of the data. Meanwhile, physicists have become impatient with the question: What is light *really*—wave or particle? Their attitude is to choose either theory according to the purposes at hand, or even to speculate with new theories, so long as the theory is not inconsistent with the practical manipulations and measurements which occur in the laboratory. There is, on the one hand, a definite body of data and certain definite procedures which can be carried out, and these exercise a "veto" over any theory from which these data and procedures are not derivable. On the other hand, there is considerable freedom in choosing a theory, or axiom system, since several alternative theories may be consistent with the data.

It is as if one were to ask: What curve is determined by

these three points (described in terms of definite positions on known axes)?

There is a great deal of freedom in choosing one's answer. No one curve is uniquely determined by these points. In fact, an infinite number of curves may be constructed so as to satisfy the conditions. Thus:

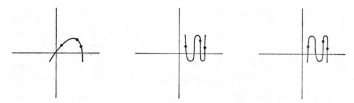

and so on.

Yet this does not mean that one may just choose any curve at all. The three given points exercise a veto over some which might be proposed. Thus:

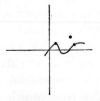

My point is simply this: it is now widely recognized in philosophy of science that although the data of experience do have a very important relation to any proposed explanation of experience, the relation is not a simple, inductive one, according to which the data uniquely determine a specific theory. Rather, the situation is more complex. So far as the negative function of ruling out a given theory is concerned, the data may have a definite and decisive role to play. As it is said, one contrary instance disproves the law. But so far as the positive function of determining the true theory is concerned, no finite set of data can uniquely determine it. The data may act as an occasion for suggesting a theory. They may confirm a theory, not in the sense of proving it to be *the true theory*, but only in the sense of being compatible with it.

This does not mean that there is an infinity of "good" theories (as there were an infinity of "good" curves in the example given above) in any complex situation. But it does mean that the finite mind, operating in finite time, must be content with something less than positive proof of a theory as the uniquely true theory.

Now, in philosophy of science, principles for choosing between competing theories (each of which is consistent with the data) have been, to a large extent, commonly agreed upon. Given two theories, each consistent with the data, that one is better which is (1) simpler, (2) more fruitful, (3) congruent with other accepted theories, and the like. These principles operate well enough so that the practical work of science can go on. However, when pressed in detail, difficulties arise. What is simplicity in a theory? Fruitful for what? What if some or all of our accepted theories are false? [4]

In the above discussion of the relation of data (experience) to theory in the field of science, I hope that I have laid a foundation for two assertions which are important for what I wish to say about theology and experience. First, nonempirical and nonlogical factors play a prominent role (even in science and much more so in a field like theology) in the selection of an explanatory theory. (This is true in spite of the fact that there are definite empirical and logical rules in science for testing the validity of a theory once adopted.) Second, in choosing between alternative theories, each of which seems consistent with such data as we have, considerations come into play which are not scientific but rather philosophic. For example, considerations such as these: What is simplicity in a theory, and why should a theory be simple anyway? What kind of data should be considered as relevant to the testing of a theory? Shall only sense data be permitted, and, if so, on what grounds? [5]

I should like now to state my own views. I am aware of the fact that the problem with which I am dealing is a vexed one and that each point which I raise deserves full discussion. As someone has said, however, if theological method is to be fully discussed, nothing else will ever get said.

I had better begin perhaps by stating my understanding of the relations between Biblical or confessional theology and philosophical theology. Of the two, confessional theology is of far greater importance for the practical life of the Church and of the believer. This kind of theology is, in the broadest sense, simply the attempt of the Church to understand and remain true to the faith of the Church. It is not an inquiry into truth—except, of course, in the sense that it is an attempt to understand something "given" which it believes to be the truth. I mean, however, that confessional theology does not seek to establish the truth in terms of some generally applicable criteria. Rather it confesses what it believes to be the truth upon which it is established. This kind of theology finds expression not only in volumes of "Church Dogmatics" but also in the liturgy and preaching of the Church, as well as in indirect though very important ways (through art and literature and through the examples of Christian lives).

I personally have no doubt that confessional theology, in this sense, is prior in many ways to philosophical theology. It is prior in experience. That is to say, the individual lives in a community of faith (not necessarily the Christian faith) before he can begin a serious philosophical inquiry into the object of faith. Otherwise, one would have a situation analogous to a person who had never been interested in and had never "seen anything in" works of art undertaking to write a philosophy of art. As St. Augustine knew, we "believe in order to understand." (However, this does not imply that the understanding which comes with inquiry may not affect belief.)

The realm of confessional theology is that of faith. That is, it seeks to confront us with what it believes to be a truth which lays upon us a claim, namely, the commitment of our whole self. Faith is more than belief, for it makes a claim not only upon the mind but upon the feeling and action of the individual. Nevertheless, one of the very important claims of faith is upon the mind. Faith includes belief.

It is important for what follows to be clear on the relation between faith and knowledge. I believe that everything is to be gained and nothing lost by limiting the concept "knowledge" to those beliefs which may be justified in terms of a method of verification which is communicable and open in principle to the understanding and criticism of any normal human being. I know that this statement bristles with difficulties. It is no doubt impossible in practice to state precisely what is meant by "verification" or "communicable" or "normal human being." It is for this reason that scientists, for example, who are especially concerned with the refinement of the tools of knowledge, have given up the ideal of certainty—except in purely formal matters.

I do not want to get into an argument over words. Some people choose to use the term knowledge differently. I feel my usage has several advantages. First, it calls attention to the great difference between accepting beliefs on the basis of tradition or personal intuition, on the one hand, and on the basis of empirical method, on the other hand. I will admit that we never find these two attitudes in a pure state.

Every empiricist in fact accepts much on the basis of tradition or hunch. And every believer in a particular tradition has to some extent sought to justify his belief in terms of his observations of the world and in terms of the beliefs of other people. Yet there is a profound difference. In terms of my inquiry, this difference can be stated with reference to the belief that God is the end or object of our desire for the good. It is one thing to believe this on the basis of one's participation in a tradition, the community of faith, or even on the basis of certain compelling personal religious experiences. It is quite a different thing to believe in this on the basis of a method by which it can in principle be shown to any person that such and such experiences, not restricted to a special group, definitely imply the belief. My own feeling is that the term knowledge has been given a relatively precise explication by empirical philosophers. It only confuses things to label as knowledge religious beliefs whose epistemological basis is quite different.

Second, my usage has the advantage of avoiding separate and different realms of knowledge. Many theologians want to claim that religious faith gives a higher or better knowledge than is available in any other way. Yet it always turns out that this higher knowledge cannot be related to anything else we call knowledge. It is personal, not describable or predictable, not verifiable. In short, it lacks the defining characteristics of knowledge as this term is ordinarily used. I would prefer simply to call this higher function "faith," or that aspect of faith which we call belief.

There is a term common to the realm of faith and the realm of knowledge: it is belief. One aspect of faith is belief. It is belief which is based upon tradition, or upon personal religious experience, or both. Such belief may, of course, be true (certainly the believer believes it to be true!); but even if it is true, it is not knowledge unless its truth can be verified or defended with reference to a public method. Knowledge is belief justified or verified by a public method.

In discussing confessional theology, I said that its realm is that of faith. It seeks to understand the beliefs of the community of faith. In a sense, therefore, this kind of theology is descriptive. Or, perhaps better, it is a proclamation for our time of what it believes and what it has received from the community of believers. This kind of theology has nothing to do with attempts to prove its beliefs in terms of more general considerations. Such theology is of utmost importance for the ongoing life of the Church. It affirms, asserts, proclaims. But—it is a setting forth of beliefs; it is not knowledge.

Insofar as theology wishes to claim that it achieves knowledge, it must enter the sphere of philosophical theology. Knowledge is all of a piece, in the sense that it all demands justification in terms of a common, human method. It may be that it is a mistake for theology ever to seek to move beyond the realm of faith. It is certainly true that attempts to justify belief in God, or in Christ, by means of an appeal to a general method of inquiry have seemed inconclusive to many people; have perhaps raised more questions than they have settled. In place of clear-cut affirmation one gets questions and problems.

In spite of this admission, however, I believe that philosophical theology is of great importance. The importance of philosophical theology is often put in terms of apologetics, that is, in terms of an effort to convince nonbelievers by argument that the belief of the Church is true. Today it has become fashionable to deride apologetics. Conversion is the work of the Holy Ghost. The Word of God can create faith without our help. No doubt! But I think that this passivity on our part is questionable even from the point of view of the Christian faith. This attitude of passivity goes along with that interpretation of Christianity which empties the historical life of man of any real significance. Why may

not the Word, or the Holy Ghost, work *through* man's efforts, including his philosophical efforts? Were men not
commissioned to preach? Of course, one could argue that
something suprahuman takes over when men begin to preach
and that, therefore, the preaching does not depend upon
normal processes of human thought. But I prefer to believe
that God can use us as instruments in preaching the Gospel
without by-passing our human characteristics.

It often seems to me, indeed, that those who demand that
all human elements be eliminated from crucial aspects of
theology betray not only a one-sided interpretation of Christianity but also a lack of faith in God. No matter how im-
perfect man or his reasoning processes may be, is not God
able to work *through* them? Indeed, I feel that there is no
escape from using our ordinary rational faculties. This is just
the human condition. Those who feel that these faculties are
by-passed are fooling themselves. To be sure, one might argue
in the abstract that an omnipotent God could plant truths
in our minds which depend in no way upon our reasoning.
But what warrant do we have for supposing that God does in
fact operate in this way? Such a mode of operation would
be, I submit, a negation of the significance of history. And,
as a matter of fact, I think it can be shown that theologians
who claim to have such privileged access to truth nevertheless reflect, when they come to state this truth, certain
philosophical biases which are prominent in their cultural
milieu. There is no escape from the human element in
theology. Therefore, the only thing to do is to admit this
element and to seek to use our reason as faithfully and
humbly as may be possible.

I am not saying that reason will ever be able to prove all
that faith wishes to believe. In fact, I do not think it will.
It will always be necessary to accept on faith much that we
cannot rationally understand. But we cannot be absolved
from the responsibility of rational judgment, so far as that
can carry us. Nor should we be blind to the fact that our

faith is, no doubt, colored to some extent by the judgments we have reached rationally.

So much by way of a general defense of philosophical theology. It is time to state how such a theology is to develop.

My view contains a strong empiricist element, but it is not to be identified with what is often called empirical theology. There are at least two significant departures from that tradition. The first has to do with the problem of induction, mentioned above (pp. 95 ff.). I do not believe that significant theological categories are to be established inductively by some process of simply inspecting experience. We do not approach experience with blank minds, empty of presuppositions. We approach it with the "eyes of faith" (whether the Christian or the naturalist or some other faith); and this depends, too, upon the history of the group which nourishes our faith. I will argue that our significant theological categories depend upon revelation.

Second, I depart from empiricism, as it is often understood, by rejecting the notion that the criterion of the truth (and meaning) of our theological categories is whether they explain our experiences. The concept of explanation has been given a fairly precise meaning in recent empiricist literature.[6] According to this view, a concept or theory explains if it enables us to predict, under given conditions, at least some *specific* details of future experience which can be deduced from the theory (or, in the case of past events, the theory would have enabled us so to predict). The point is that an explanatory concept or theory definitely implies certain specific events which, if they do not occur, are capable of refuting the theory. It is because this concept of empirical explanation was applied to theological concepts that we had all the discussion on the topic: can "God" be disconfirmed? The assumption was that if "God" cannot, in theory, be disconfirmed, then "He" does not imply anything specific and, thus, is a vacuous or meaningless concept. This is the line of reasoning behind John Wisdom's complaint against theology, mentioned above (p. 94).

But it is, I believe, a mistake to think of theological concepts exactly on the analogy of physical concepts—where, of course, the notion of explanation has its rightful home. A closer analogy is with philosophical concepts, where we have not explanation but "interpretation." There are, for example, certain time-honored philosophical theories which have an empirical base and reference and yet which fail of any explanatory power in the sense given above. But they do serve to interpret our experience, not perhaps this or that specific detail of experience, but a complex wealth of interrelated experiences. Take, for example, the philosophical doctrine of mind-body dualism. This doctrine interprets a whole congeries of interrelated experiences having to do with our mental life in its relations to bodily events. The interpretation embodied in this doctrine is significantly different from that embodied in the doctrine of nondualism. Yet I think anyone would be hard put to cite one concrete bit of data (that is, a specific detail of experience) which one theory could explain and the other could not. At least some of the serious proponents of each theory are acquainted with all of the relevant facts known to the other side. But the difference of interpretation remains.

This situation does mean, it seems to me, that these two philosophical interpretations are (at present) vacuous so far as the ongoing work of biology and of psychology is concerned. If one's concern is with a given empirical *science*, the interpretations neither add nor subtract from one's results. They are not fruitful for further experimentation. But it does not follow that these interpretations are in every sense vacuous. They make a difference to man's self-understanding at the philosophical level.

Furthermore, two such divergent interpretations may persist because each is relatively successful in interpreting the facts of experience thus far known. Yet in the case of dualism and nondualism, it may well be that there are facts which, if known, would swing the balance toward one or the other theory (for example, if it could be shown that there are parapsychological phenomena such as telepathy). My point is simply that philosophy seeks a much wider generalization than do specific sciences. And it is, therefore, more complexly or loosely related to any particular fact. But this does not mean that it is unrelated to the facts of experience altogether. The situation might be portrayed on some such scale as the following:

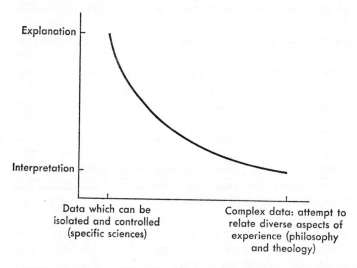

Thus I do not want to say that explanation and interpretation are utterly different in principle. Each seeks in some way to take account of the world of experience. But somewhere along the line, as we become more concerned to relate complex and diverse types of experience to each other (e.g., man's physical, aesthetic, and ethical relations to another human being), it becomes less possible to construct an explanation and more necessary to rely upon an interpretation. It is my feeling that theological concepts offer an interpretation of our experience. It would be shortsighted to reject theology because it does not explain the specific details of experience, as we now understand these details. And it would, I think, be equally wrongheaded to say that experience has no function in the work of theology simply because the relation cannot be exhibited in terms of various detailed explanations.

I wish to stress that interpretation is continuous with explanation. This implies that experience does, though in a looser way than in the special sciences, exercise a control in determining which interpretation is warranted. This, in turn, implies that all the discussion about "disconfirming God" is not pointless. The error has been in expecting confirmation or disconfirmation by means of specific details, such as might be predicted by a scientific explanation, rather than a looser but nevertheless real congruity or incongruity between an interpretation and experience as a whole. One point of John Wisdom's article is that no theist permits the facts concerning specific evils in life to count against his belief. Yet I think it is not true that experience as a whole could be of any character whatsoever without affecting theistic belief. Furthermore, I have the feeling that the latitude within which theistic belief can survive, at least without evident fanaticism, is not as great as one might suppose. If evil were in greater preponderance, and if (to cite a few instances of the kind of experience which I would regard as relevant) prayer were always barren, and if neither in our generation nor others did we find examples of lives morally transformed and creative, theistic belief would be a poor interpretation of our experience—and would, I think, be felt by most people to be such.

EXPERIENCE, REVELATION, AND REASON

The ground must be prepared in our general human experience for any special, revelatory awareness of God. There must be, as Rudolf Bultmann has put it (see pp. 130-133), some "prior understanding" of God before revelation can be received. I am convinced that the only way to avoid this conclusion is the way of Karl Barth. And this is to introduce a radical discontinuity into human life. It is to separate the man of faith from mankind generally and from history. (See Ch. VIII). But such a radical discontinuity seems contrary not only to common sense but to Scripture itself.[7]

By a prior understanding I do not mean that our general experience gives us a clear concept of God, much less "saving knowledge" of Him. I simply mean that one must have some experience of and notion (however implicit) of good and evil, of death, of guilt and forgiveness, before the Word of the Gospel can be heard and understood. The notion of a prior understanding simply suggests that God reaches us *in and through* the created world and our experience of it, and not by some miraculous invasion which is unconnected with our former lives.

More specifically, we have a prior understanding of God in the sense of our desire for God (though this may be implicit and not formulated in terms of the concept God). In this specific sense our prior understanding, if it were to be made explicit, would take the form of the Augustinian "Thou hast made us for Thyself, and our hearts are restless till they rest in Thee."

Our anxiety over death or guilt is such a prior understanding. For at these points of our human experience, an implicit and often explicit search for eternal life and forgiveness and perfect righteousness takes shape. This is not to say that a revealed Word from God tells us exactly the same thing as we had understood for ourselves on the basis of our reflection on our experience. But if such a Word is to reach us, if it is to have any meaning for us, it must speak to the questions we had already been aware of.

A person comes to know, in a general way, that we all must die. He sees dead animals and dead people. He is told by someone who has been through it that the death of someone very close and deeply loved is a shattering experience. He imagines that he understands this: "It must be like losing part of oneself," he says. But only when this happens to him does he *really* understand. Now, on the one hand, the event, when it occurs, speaks to him something which he could not imagine and certainly not fully understand. But, on the other hand, if when the loved one died he had no background of experience with death at all, he would be prevented from grasping what had really happened. He might suppose he was seeing a curious form of sleep, or that the person would get up tomorrow morning. He might be bewildered, shocked, strangely moved. But without a prior understanding there would be in this event no Word for him.

Revelation is, itself, a kind of experience. Something happens to us. It differs from other experiences in being *crucial*. Something happens which we had not, could not have, anticipated—and it transforms the way in which we look at things. In Israel there was a prior understanding of redemption and of the Messiah. *Some kind* of divine action was awaited. But no one could foresee specifically what did happen. What did happen made contact with the prior understanding, but transformed it.

The immediate and ultimate source of the Christian interpretation of life is revelation. It is what happened in and through Jesus the Christ. Since the time of Christ, the memory of Him and the teaching about Him have become part of the prior understanding of those of us raised in the Christian tradition—and, to some extent, of everyone in western culture. This revelation has, as it were, left an historical deposit. But for us, no less than for the first Christians, this revelation must become personal and immediate before it really speaks to and interprets our experience.

The theologian does not begin to interpret human experience generally in a presuppositionless way. He speaks from within that interpretation which emerges from revelation. But just as the original revelation is not divorced from experience, so the categories and doctrines of the theologian offer an interpretation of human experience. Theology, thus, arises within experience, is shaped primarily by a *crucial* experience, and retains its validity only if it indeed interprets experience.

Theology is thus continuous with other rational activities. It is different from science, or artistic interpretation, because its fundamental, organizing insight springs from a special, crucial experience. And this experience is something that *has happened*, not something arrived at by inductive generalization. But, like other rational activities, it goes on to interpret human experience in the light of its fundamental postulate. It offers an understanding of why human life is as it is.

The Role of Experience

I have suggested several ways in which experience plays a role in theology: in terms of what I have called a prior understanding, in terms of the crucial experience or reception of revelation, and in terms of the material which is interpreted by revelation. Actually, as I suggest in my critical comment on Barth's notion that man is entirely passive in receiving revelation, it is not possible, I think, to separate these three items so neatly. In speaking of revelation, it is no doubt important to stress that something happens which we had not anticipated. We are confronted. Yet in every process of perception, and no less in the perception of such a complex event as Christ, the human mind, out of past experience, contributes something to the understanding of the event. What we hear or see is, to some extent, influenced by past experience, by expectations, and by the ideas of our culture. It is for this reason that not all men, not even all Christians, understand the Word of revelation in the same way. Insofar as theology is the expression of our understanding of revelation, it is in this respect also like other

rational activities. It is beset by differences of interpretation. It cannot eliminate the human factor from the interpretation of what has happened. Though we may, and must
if we are Christians, believe that something definite has
happened in which God has revealed himself, theology itself
never becomes infallible. We believe that God is there, but
our speaking of this reflects the relativities of our diverse
experiences. There is no escape from this situation for mortal
man. He can only try, as honestly as he may, to test the
adequacy of what he says in his theology in terms of his
crucial experience and also his general experience.

ADEQUACY OF INTERPRETATION

Earlier I raised the question as to whether experience
generally, or the experience of anxiety in particular, can help
in the discrimination of better from worse theology. What
role does experience play in determining the adequacy of
a theological doctrine? I want now to state my answer to
this question, and then to illustrate it with reference to my
inquiry into anxiety.

The test of the adequacy of a theology, like the test for
any theoretical concept or system, is how well it "saves
the appearances." That is, it must, first of all, account for
experience. The theory must be such that, assuming its
truth, it would (1) not lead us to expect events which are
contradicted by our experience, and (2) help us to understand why our experience in the relevant domain has the
characteristics it does have.[8]

It might seem at first that the above assertion applies only
to philosophical and not to confessional theology. But it
applies even to the latter—only in this case the appearances
or experiences considered are constituted by the crucial experience, revelation. Confessional theology does, however,
introduce a theoretical element; it puts forward a systematic
interpretation of why this crucial experience is as it is and
how it is related to our life. If this were not so, the Church

would be content with the reading and contemplation of Scripture. The crucial experience is certainly portrayed there —and more movingly than in any theology. But it is not systematic enough to fulfill our interest in a theoretical interpretation of our important experiences.

Theology differs from philosophy not in the canons of rational judgment which apply but in the fundamental postulate (and area of concern) determined by a certain crucial experience. I want to argue, therefore, that it is not open to theology any more than philosophy to save the appearances in any old way. The first test of adequacy is whether the theory can save the appearances. But there are other tests, of which two are most important and most generally accepted. These other tests bring to bear upon the theory, in addition to the question of empirical adequacy (can it save the appearances?), considerations as to its consistency and its simplicity.

Of two theories, each of which can save the appearances with equal success, that one is better which is simpler. I mentioned above (p. 99) that the concept of simplicity is not very simple if we probe it enough. Yet the point made here is certainly a valid one. To cite an example from the history of science, the Ptolemaic theory of astronomy was never disproven in the sense that it could be shown not to save the appearances. But it was abandoned because, as more data came in, it was necessary to make the theory ever more complex in order to be compatible with experience.

Again, a theory must be consistent in two senses. It must contain no logical contradictions within the system. And it must be consistent with other generally accepted theories. In theology this would mean that there can be no formal inconsistencies in the theological system. And also, any particular doctrine must be consistent with other relevant knowledge. Consistency with other relevant knowledge is no doubt an ideal criterion which in many cases it would be problematical to apply—since, often, the relevant knowledge would consist in a philosophical doctrine which itself is much under debate. But the criterion of consistency within the theological system itself is by no means an empty one, as (for example) Gustaf Wingren has shown in his recent work, *Theology in Conflict*.

I am not suggesting that these criteria—which might be called empirical application, simplicity, and consistency —are tools that are completely understood or easy to use. But I do believe that they are the tools of all human thinking, insofar as it seeks to be rational. And this applies to theology, too.

It could be shown, I believe, where both the Barthian and the Thomistic doctrines run afoul of these criteria at certain points. I want to illustrate this in the case of the Barthian theology, taking as the appearances which are to be saved the phenomena of anxiety.

The analyses of anxiety by people of various backgrounds and from different points of view all suggest the same conclusion: anxiety presupposes an awareness of and desire for a "good" the attainment of which is, however, threatened. In the case of religious anxiety, some awareness of and desire for God appear to be involved. In fact, my inquiry in the early chapters might be regarded as an extended footnote to St. Augustine's "Thou has made us for Thyself, and our hearts are restless till they rest in Thee." The appearance which is to be saved, then, is a human desire for God which is manifest in our anxieties. Any adequate theology must account for this experience in some way.

In this case, the simplest doctrine or theory would be one which accepted these appearances in a relatively straightforward way. This might be done through the scholastic doctrine of a natural desire for God. In any case, some doctrine of man's condition seems to be called for which allows for a very general urge to seek God. In the concluding chapter, I shall suggest an approach to the appearances through the Christian doctrine of the image of God.

Barth, however, cannot permit any such simple theory, for his whole theology is based upon the assumption of an antithesis between God and "natural" man. Natural man is totally depraved. For Barth, as for the reformers, this stress on man's depravity is a protest against the tendency to minimize man's need for grace. Barth seems to assume that if we allow any degree of natural awareness of or desire for God, there is a danger of supposing that we can dispense with revelation and grace. I do not believe that this is true at all. I have pointed out above (pp. 79-80) that it is not true for Thomas Aquinas, though there are tendencies in that direction. Gustaf Wingren has shown, in his able criticism of Barth, that this is not true for the Bible. According to Wingren, Barth's theology is dominated by the problem of knowledge. In this he is a modern and does not share the view of the Bible. The Biblical drama, according to Barth, is that, before the revelation in Christ, man has absolutely no knowledge of God and that, with that revelation, knowledge is given. But, as Wingren points out, this is a very forced reading of the Bible.

Man's predicament is not that he lacks knowledge, but that he is guilty. He is guilty because he knew what he ought to do, but he pursued his own works against God.[9]

Wingren goes on:

When the idea of revelation becomes the governing point of view, man's realization of the revelation becomes in fact the dominant point of view. But if God's activity is permitted to occupy the center, there is every reason to speak of God's work in creation even before the gospel.[10]

I think this is a very damaging charge against Barth. In his eagerness to protect the principle of grace and to stress man's desperate need, Barth has outdone the Bible; has, in fact, distorted the Scriptural view. And this is very seri-

ous for a theologian who claims to take the Bible as his
controlling norm.

My point is twofold. Barth rejects the simple theory because it conflicts with his basic assumption. But it turns out
that his pursuit of his basic assumption leads him to an
inner conflict, to a conflict with another of his basic assumptions. Second, he still has to account for the appearance that man desires God. And this he must do, given his
postulate of depravity, in a highly complex way. It is necessary for him to explain all apparent desire for God as (1)
either an illusion, or (2) as a result of grace received through
Christ. But this leaves no way of knowing when man's apparent desire for God is actually a subtle form of self-seeking
and when it is a result of grace.

It is much better to abandon the postulate of total depravity, and to benefit from a simpler doctrine, particularly
since the postulate of depravity leads to conflict within the
theological system itself. Such considerations as these simply
illustrate the application of the criteria for determining a
better from a worse theory. They are, of course, human criteria, and therefore, the Barthians will not be much im-
pressed. Nevertheless, I argue that there is finally no escape
from such rational judgment (except, of course, just to
cease writing theology and let the Gospel speak for itself),
and that the application of such criteria does not prevent
us from remaining as close to the Biblical point of view as
those who disdain such considerations. I believe that it is
possible to save the appearances of the phenomena of anxiety by means of a simpler and more direct doctrine, and a
doctrine which is rooted in the Biblical concept of the
image of God (see Chapter IX).

THE MEDIATING ROLE OF EXPERIENCE

Often a situation arises in theology in which a salutary
effect may be realized by taking seriously the responsibility
of theology for interpreting the data of experience. There

is a tendency, due largely to historical exigencies, for theology to be determined too largely by polemical considerations. This is exactly what happened in the Reformation period with reference to many doctrines. In particular, the doctrine of man (and of the image of God in man) was crystallized in two opposing views, each of which was in large part determined by the struggle against the opponent. Thus we have the spectacle of two groups within the Christian tradition, each claiming the authority of Scripture, asserting opposite things about man. One group asserts that he has a natural virtue and desire for God, the other that he is totally depraved and the image of God rendered a completely ineffectual relic.

Such polemical opposites can, I am convinced, be mediated if we take seriously the obligation of theology to make sense out of man's actual experience. This may be seen in two ways. First, even at the time when the polemical fight was fiercest, it was necessary for each side to introduce certain "distinctions" into their theologies in order not to violate too flagrantly the facts of experience. And these distinctions had the effect of softening the opposition, of bringing into view certain common-sense considerations recognized by both sides. Thus the Catholic theologians stressed that the Fall of man left the image of God intact. But how, then, account for the persistence of sin and the apparent need for grace? Well, it was necessary to introduce a distinction. The image of God is retained but the likeness is lost. Furthermore, the image is weakened by sin. Such qualifications prepare for the serious discussion by Catholic theologians of the effects of sin and the need for grace.

Or one can illustrate this same tendency from the other side. The Calvinists insisted upon man's total depravity. But how, then, account for certain signs of the nobility of man, such as his intellectual capacities and his moral impulses? Well, some distinctions are called for. In fact, the Calvinist divines tended to produce a bewildering and complex set of distinctions, in order to protect their doctrine and yet admit the ordinary goodness of man. Thus, it was said that the essence of the image of God remains after the Fall, but that its powers are entirely lost. Or it was said that even after the Fall, man is supported by "common grace," which enables him to attain to moral and civic virtue, but that he has utterly lost that "special grace of the Holy Spirit" by which alone it would be possible to act in a way pleasing to God.[11] Such distinctions are introduced to accommodate the evident facts of experience, that there is in man an awareness of and desire for the good; and insofar as experience compels the introduction of such qualifying distinctions, conversation (as against mere polemics) between the diverse theological traditions becomes possible.

It is my belief that an understanding of our experiences of anxiety may, in a fruitful way, mediate between the doctrines of natural desire and total depravity. In so doing, it may also suggest a new approach to the traditional Christian doctrine of the image of God which I shall discuss in the final chapter.

VIII

Anxiety and the Word:
THE POSITION OF KARL BARTH

There are two interrelated reasons why a somewhat more detailed examination of the position of Karl Barth may be helpful. First, his theology constitutes a denial of my suggestion that a desire for God remains, even in natural man. Second, he would support the conclusion of certain positivistic philosophers that theology is not influenced by an analysis of experience.

Such a conclusion, that the nature of experience has no real influence upon theology, would not disturb a Barthian, or anyone who holds that revelation alone and in itself determines the content of doctrine. A Barthian would, however, object to the notion that this renders theology meaningless. True theology is what is spoken *to* man, from beyond the circle of his experience. Theology does not need to be confirmed from experience, as if light is shed upon the meaning of God from man's life. The situation is rather the reverse, that what is revealed shines in its own light and gives meaning *to* experiences which previously were inchoate and capable, so far as man's knowledge is concerned, of diverse, relative interpretations.

Barth's position in this matter depends upon both a radical skepticism with regard to ordinary human knowledge and a radical realism with regard to that knowledge which is given in revelation. Reasoning on the basis of human experience, man can only discover relations within his experience, relations dependent, furthermore, upon his particular vantage point in time, space, and culture. In the realm of religion, all knowledge based upon man's religious experience is really only knowledge of himself, of his fears and desires, though man wishes to pretend it is more.[1] In short, so far as *general* theory of knowledge is concerned, Barth is in thorough agreement with modern empiricism, even positivism, though he personally derives this point of view from the Kantian rather than the empiricist tradition. All knowledge, so far as it is won by human reflection, is based upon and conditioned by experience; therefore, it can never reach beyond experience. It is always knowledge of relations within the world, of immanence.

Nevertheless, according to Barth, there is a kind of knowledge which is absolute, which tells of what transcends the world (God). How can such a contention be made, in view of what has just been said about human knowledge? This can be said because the knowledge of revelation is not human; it is entirely determined by God in His freedom; man is *entirely* passive; he only receives this divine Word.[2] The sole acting subject in this knowledge is the second person of the Trinity, Jesus Christ as the Word of God. One might with justice say that, according to Barth, man contributes nothing to the process of revelation except that he is its locus.

To be sure, once man is *determined by* the Word of God, he has "an experience of the Word of God." But Barth is careful to guard against the notion that this experience stands independently as something from which the existence or the nature of the Word of God can be inferred.

. . . a determination of man's existence by the Word of God . . . is not to be confused with any sort of determination which man can give to his own existence. . . . No determination which man can give himself is as such determination by the

Word of God. But neither can there be room here for the other
view, as if in this experience it were a case of co-operation
between divine determination and human self-determination.
. . . If a man lets himself be told by the Word of God that
he has a Lord, that he is His creature, a lost sinner in receipt
of grace . . . then this particular content of the experienced
Word will flatly forbid him to ascribe to himself, wholly or in
part, the possibility of such experience or even to equate dialectically with a possibility proper to himself the divine possibility which is realized in such experience.[3]

Nothing could be a flatter rejection of the notion that
theology can gain anything of importance from an analysis
of human experience for its concept of the relation between
God and man. There is no structure of human experience
which even discloses the *possibility* of a relation to God.
*The possibility of knowing God is created new in the mo-
ment in which God makes himself known.*

All of the above does not mean, however, that such a
theology can give no account of human experience. It only
means that general experience is prevented from assuming
any role as a criterion of truth. If and when God does
reveal Himself, however, He does so concretely to individual
men. He enters into and determines their experience. From
the point of view of having received the Word of God, one
could then proceed to describe how this illumines experience.

In terms of my inquiry, the import of Barth's position can
be stated quite simply. From the character of man's anxieties we can learn nothing about God, either about whether
he exists or how he is related to man. But from being transformed, illumined, determined by the Word of God, we
can come to understand our anxieties. Thus the Word of
God with its message, Barth would insist, of total depravity
must stand as the fixed point in all our reasoning about
anxiety. I have suggested above (pp. 87 ff.) how the

phenomena of anxiety would be viewed from this vantage point.

It must be said that Barth's position has great strength. Not only has it called attention to the dangers of allowing theology to be determined by modern culture, but it has a power of replying to certain kinds of criticism which find favor today. Specifically, I mentioned above the current popular criticism of theology; namely, that it is meaningless because one cannot specify experiences which either confirm or disconfirm its propositions. Granting Barth's position, this is exactly what we should expect to be the case. There is a curious underlying affinity at this point between Barth and our contemporary empiricists. If Barth is to be attacked, it must be on a deeper level than a mere complaint that one cannot establish theological doctrines by a rational scrutiny of human experience.

In a sense, I am diffident about the criticisms of Barth which I shall now offer. For all of them presuppose that there is no form of knowledge whatsoever, including revelation, in which the human subject remains completely passive. To put this in a different way, I will assume that some elements of human selectivity and interpretation enter into any intelligible view of the nature of things, and that this holds true even when that view is apparently *given* to the individual. The individual selects from what is given, and also adds to it in interpretation. If Barth, or anyone else, should object that I am here speaking not of revelation itself but of human theological systems, I would reply that my strictures hold also of revelation if it has any cognitive import.

It may be possible to distinguish between experience and interpretation. One might argue (though I am not sure how truthfully) that there are moments in which one is related to something beyond the self in a totally passive way, moments in which one merely sees, hears, is open to the "being" of the other in terms of *its,* and not in any degree of one's own, qualities. If this can be done, it would be possible to say that there is a purely passive way in which humans can be related to other things, and perhaps then also to a divine Other. But such a moment of pure openness or receptivity, if it does exist, would not have a cognitive character; it would certainly not be a Word imparting knowledge. For as soon as the Word said anything definite it would stress this or that aspect of the experience; it would select from the experience itself. What I am saying is that all human knowledge is discursive, mediated by symbols, selective. It does not help to confuse raw experience, if there is such a thing, with knowledge. To be open to the concrete fullness of something may be, and undoubtedly is, more important than knowledge of it; but that does not make it knowledge.

Therefore, I would have to say to Barth that either there is no such event as a revelation in which man is totally passive or, if there is, it is something of the order of a raw experience, a just-being-confronted by something new, which as yet has no Word for us. I know that Barth says that the revealing event, Christ, does not give us information; rather, it gives us Christ Himself. Very well, the event (or the experience), before interpretation, just is itself. And it may be a transforming, crucial event. But it is not knowledge until it is interpreted. As soon as the event bears a Word, in any ordinary sense of telling us something about God or about ourselves, it has been clothed with human interpretations.[4]

As a matter of fact, I am more radically skeptical about the possibility of a humanly uninterpreted Word than the above might suggest. For I doubt that the way in which any human being is capable of receiving any impression or experience is unaffected by his past experience and training. Of course, Barth might and does argue that God breaks through, overwhelms, such selective predispositions. When God speaks in Christ, He, at the same moment, creates in the hearer a new disposition which is not of himself or his culture but of God. This is a heroic solution of the problem which has the effect of nullifying the significance of human nature, of culture, and of history.[5] Or, to put it in another way, this solution destroys the unity of mankind: man before and after the Fall, and before and after redemption, just is not the same being.

This is not a conclusive point, but it is interesting to note that Barth understands the Word in accordance with the particular traditions in which he was reared; and his understanding is at variance with that of other men who are, so far as we have any way of knowing, also Christian.

My point, then, is that no theological position is simply received passively. I do believe that men may be, in a very real sense, *confronted* by Christ. But there is no way at all for men to avoid the processes of human thought when they try to understand the meaning of that event. Of course, in a sense Barth admits that the processes of human thought are involved. But he holds that they *may* be involved, in the case of a true "theology of the Word," in a very special way which is really entirely different from what we would ordinarily mean by this. That is, human thought processes may be involved, but so dominated and determined by divine grace that their particular mode of operation and their conclusions are not even a possibility for man as such, apart from the invasion of grace.[6] Again we come to the monism in which God is all and man nothing.

For me to point out that this monism is involved in Barth's position is not to refute it. More consistently than one would believe possible, Barth defends this position at all points. I do not believe he can be refuted. But I do believe that the implications of his position can be laid bare. Beyond this it is possible to raise other critical questions. Is his position really, as he would insist, faithful to the Biblical view? From the point of view of ordinary human canons of thought, is not his position either trivial or false? Does not his position drive him, in order to be consistent, into other grave theological difficulties? And, finally, is his position necessary in order to protect what he and his tradition (and this would have to be determined by historical analysis) really regard as central to the Christian faith? I shall address myself briefly to each of these questions.

With regard to Barth's faithfulness to the Biblical view I have little to say, as I am hardly a competent judge. My impression, however, is that one has to take history much more seriously than does Barth in order to represent the Biblical attitude. He seems to rob man and history of any independent, even if created, significance. It is as if, after the Fall, the whole drama of history is a dumb show—except where, in a totally unexpected and unexpectable way, a bolt of revelation is shot down by God. And the revealing event, itself, is strangely anhistorical. Richard R. Niebuhr is, I believe, right in his analysis of Barth's un-Biblical position on this point.[7]

Is Barth's view not either trivial or false? I think it can be shown to be so. However, I must warn that this criticism is a philosophical one which, as such, would carry little weight with Barth or his followers. It has weight, however, if I am right in my argument (see above) that not even theology can avoid involvement in ordinary human thought processes.

What I want to show here may first be suggested by an analogy, which is very closely related to our theme. The analogy is the discussion in ethics of the position of egoistic hedonism. Such a hedonist as Hobbes would hold that *every* human action is undertaken out of a selfish motive. I think that contemporary philosophical analysis can show that such a position is either trivial or false. For suppose we point to an act which appears to be altruistic—a starving mother gives her last morsel of food to her starving child. The hedonist does not deny that such acts occur. But apparently such an act proves his position false. His only escape is to say that although the act *appeared* to be altruistic, really the mother desired (say) to be well thought of, and this selfish desire explains her action. The point is that the hedonist, if he is to maintain his position, is driven to permit no possible evidence to refute it. However many exceptions may be adduced, he affirms an explanation in terms of his principle. I believe that we must conclude that this renders his position trivial, for it tells us nothing whatsoever about why things are one way rather than another. His position is, in fact, analytic, that is, it depends upon the game of definition. He has determined, by definition, that any act, if it is a human act, is *eo ipso* selfish. This is why he feels there *must* be a selfish motive in every case, even though it is completely hidden.

Barth's theology is, I believe, involved in just such an analytic triviality, and this is so just because he has placed the fundamental category of revelation beyond any conceivable relation to experience. It is a category which is affirmed no matter what occurs or seems to occur. I am not speaking of the general idea of revelation but of the specifically Christian revelation.

Bound up with Barth's idea of revelation is the "otherness" of God. If man seems to have arrived by his own thought at a concept of God, it is not really a concept of God but of something else—e.g., his own ideals. For God is wholly other.

Also bound up with his idea of revelation, and more to the point in our discussion, is the conviction that man is totally depraved. If someone *seems* to desire God, he really desires only self-glorification. For man is totally depraved. This kind of tautologous thinking is rendered more complex, however, by the recognition that man's depravity may be overcome by grace. So, if one seems to desire God, either this is an illusion or the individual has received special divine grace. But no evidence is allowed to count against the doctrine of total depravity. If one should argue that a Hindu saint, who had never heard of Christ, in fact loved God,

Karl Barth would not feel that he had to examine the evidence at all in order to reply. Either the man is fooling himself and others or he has received the grace of Christ. The principle is not at all responsive to the course of human experience. From the ordinary human point of view, therefore, it is trivial. It tells us nothing in detail about why things are one way rather than another. It is isolated from the rest of the intellectual life of man.

Of course, I am here using profane arguments. In a sense, Barth is not touched by them, for he would not deny that from a profane perspective the claims of revelation seem questionable. That some reality or relation may, indeed, exist which escapes profane reasoning is not difficult to imagine. I am simply trying to point out two things. Any such reality or relation does not in any way come within the realm of knowledge. And, furthermore, to place the object of faith in such an isolated realm, while it may seem to release faith from the perils of criticism, carries with it perils of its own. It lifts the life of faith out of the stream of history. The man who is redeemed is not flesh at all.

Placing the life of faith beyond criticism would seem to carry dangers for the theologian as well. It is sometimes said that it is prideful to try to think about revelation in terms of other knowledge. I wonder if it may not be a truer humility to recognize that for man, even for the Christian man, there is no escape from the limits of historical existence and no escape from the necessity of relying to some degree on the processes by which historical, fleshly beings are fitted to arrive at judgments.

I have already suggested a few points at which Barth's position raises other grave theological problems. Barth is, I think, very successful in remaining consistently loyal to the principle of the sole efficacy of divine grace and of the total depravity of man. But this drives him into the difficulties which Calvinists have always faced. He strives hard, for example, to avoid the consequence that man is reduced to a cipher. Yet there remains a serious question whether he is successful. Regarding man's reception of the Word of God, for example, Barth wishes to say that man receives it in his self-determination; that is, that the reception of grace does not violate man's freedom. Yet this self-determination is completely determined by God. Determination by God happens *to* man's self-determination, but man's self-determination contributes nothing whatsoever to the process.[8] Nor can man of himself determine whether he will accept the Word of God; that, too, is determined by God.

> The Word of God comes as a summons to him, and the hearing which he gives it is the right hearing of obedience or the wrong hearing of disobedience. Whether it is ultimately the one or the other, does not, of course, lie within his province. To that, the obedience or disobedience of his action, he cannot resolve and determine himself.[9]

In short, Barth's consistent emphasis on man's depravity involves him in what I would regard as the danger of a rigidly monistic divine determinism. God becomes the sole actor in the drama of sin and salvation to such an extent that it is hard to avoid the judgment that God is playing with human history, giving man the illusion of involvement in issues of ultimate destiny but in reality by-passing man in His control of events and persons.

Finally, it is necessary to appreciate the evangelical motive behind all of Barth's theology and to raise the question whether his characteristic doctrines are necessary to that determining motive. It is true not only of Barth, but of the reformers, that the fundamental and central concern is with God's action in Christ. This is evangelical in that it accurately reflects the mood of the New Testament, with its "good news" that God had reconciled us "while we were yet sinners." The Christian faith is, first of all, something received. It depends not upon our striving but upon something which happens to us and for us. God takes the initiative. He receives unworthy men.

For Barth, this gospel is primary. In this sense, he is indeed a Biblical theologian. For him, as also for the reformers, the doctrines of predestination, depravity, and the like are to be understood as ways of protecting this fundamental religious, evangelical truth.

For it has happened again and again in the history of the Church that talk of man's natural desire or his natural virtue has led to a softening or even an abandonment of the evangelical position. As we saw above (p. 85), Luther links the notion of natural virtue with blindness to the grace of Christ. If man desires God, as a matter of nature, why is Christ's sacrifice necessary? Doctrines of natural virtue or natural desire suggest that man is already on his way to God; that God does little more than meet him halfway. Barth is quite right, I think, that such a view does violence to the New Testament experience and faith.

However, I should like to suggest that a concept of natural desire need not involve a weakening of the evangelical position and, as a corollary, that the doctrine of total depravity is not necessary to protect it. I have already pointed out that the emphasis on total depravity leads to its own difficulties. If it is not necessary, it should be abandoned.

That a doctrine of total depravity has seemed necessary at times is due, I believe, to historical rather than theoretical circumstances. Thus the medieval Church, which taught that man has natural virtue and natural desire, also developed certain institutional practices which suggested that man could, in part, "earn" his own salvation by his own merit, independent of grace. Yet, it seems to me, a theologian such as Thomas Aquinas, who defends the notion of natural desire, makes it perfectly plain that man can in no wise merit salvation apart from the grace of Christ.[10] In fighting against the practical implications of the sacramental system, as then popularly understood, Luther and others felt it necessary to reject a theological doctrine which was, no doubt, linked in popular thinking with the "abuses" but which, in terms of its own logic, did not imply those abuses. However much Luther's protest was historically needful, it did not dispose of the Thomistic doctrine of natural desire. Indeed, I am inclined to say that Luther, absorbed with the practical situation, did not rightly understand the intent and the limits of the doctrine as developed by Thomas himself.

Similarly, in modern times, Protestant theologians have been much enamored of the goodness and rationality of man. Such optimistic judgments in fact went along with a tendency to reject a decisive revelation or a decisive need for grace. Barth's protest was and is historically justified. But it does not follow from this that all concepts of a desire for God which is natural to man lead to the dangers which Barth battles against. Just as it was possible for a Thomas Aquinas to hold a concept of natural desire in his day, without endangering the concept of grace, so it is possible in our time.

I do not mean to suggest that we ought simply to reassert the Thomistic doctrines. Actually, it seems to me, the Thomistic concept of natural desire is perhaps more open to unevangelical distortions than need be the case; and this is due to the "models" which are taken as analogous to this desire (see pp. 136-141).

THE SIGNIFICANCE OF RUDOLF BULTMANN

One further criticism of Barth's position has to be mentioned. It has been raised by many people, but I shall present it as it appears in the writings of Rudolf Bultmann. For this criticism may at the same time serve as an introduction to a very brief discussion of Bultmann's position.

The criticism may be stated in summary form: unless man has some positive basis in his life, even before revelation, for understanding God and His will, then the Word of God, once it comes, can have no meaning for him. It is important to see what is at stake here, and to see what is implied by Barth's defense against such an objection. If there were not, the criticism runs, some human awareness of the nature of God, then no Word could be understood as the Word *of God* (rather than, say, a tempting word of Satan).

. . . *the comprehension of records about events as the action of God* presupposes a prior understanding of what may . . . be termed the action of God. . . . In human existence an *existentiell* knowledge about God is alive in the form of the inquiry about "happiness," "salvation," the meaning of the world and of history; and in the inquiry into the real nature of each person's particular "being." . . .

Existentiell knowledge about God exists *in some kind* of explicit form, when it gains conscious expression. For example, if it is consciously expressed in the question "What must I do to be saved?" (Acts 16:30), then in it some kind of notion of "salvation" is presupposed.[11]

Bultmann's position, which is explicitly developed into a criticism of Barth,[12] reflects his general principles for interpreting any historical documents.

The presupposition of every comprehending interpretation is *a previous living relationship to the subject*, which directly or indirectly finds expression in the text and which guides the direction of the enquiry.[13]

What is said in the text must be understood in the light of our own experience with the categories in which it deals.

Such an investigation is always guided by a prior understanding of "human being"—by a particular understanding of existence, which may be very naïve, but from which in general in the first instance the categories develop, which make an investigation possible. . . . Without such a *prior understanding* and the questions initiated by it, the texts are mute.[14]

These general considerations, according to Bultmann, apply

no less to the understanding of the Biblical texts and to the
processes by which man comes to understand a revelation
of God.[15]

And if this is countered by saying that neither can man know
who God is before his manifestation . . . then we have to
reply that *man may very well be aware who God is, namely,
in the inquiry about him.* If his existence were not motivated
(whether consciously or *unawares*) by the inquiry about God
in the sense of the Augustinian *"Tu nos fecisti ad Te, et cor
nostrum inquietum est, donec requiescat in Te"* then neither
would he know God as God in any manifestation of him.[16]

It is easy to see that Bultmann's thesis parallels our own: if
man did not inquire after God, in the Augustinian sense, if
his heart were not restless for God, if he had no anxious
desire for God, then he could neither understand nor relate
himself in any human way to any manifestation of God.
There must be what Bultmann calls a "prior understanding"
of revelation within human experience, and the revelation,
if and when it comes, must bear a positive relation to the
categories of that experience.

Again, as always, it must be admitted that the Barthian
has a reply; but again we may point up, from a new angle,
the implications of that reply. The reply is simply that Bultmann is talking about understanding records of historical
events "in general." There is no reason why the events of
divine revelation should be related to us in the same way.
For Barth there is no prior understanding. There is not even,
as we will recall, a possibility of anticipating the Word of
revelation. *The possibility of knowing God is created new in
the moment when God makes himself known.* Man, with his
ordinary canons of interpretation, is entirely passive in this
revealing event.

Barth's reply, I believe, is the only one that can be made
by one who wishes to deny human anticipations of the re-

lationship and knowledge of faith. But this reply entails once more what we have found again and again in our discussion of Barth: the life of faith is totally separated from human life generally. It becomes a sacred and isolated island. One can hardly refrain from saying once again: in this view, the man who is redeemed is not really man. Continuity with mankind and history, with the conditions of human existence, is completely sundered.

The significance of Bultmann is not confined to his criticisms of Barth. He is raising in a fresh way the very question now before us: How is theological doctrine related to experience? As is well known, Bultmann feels that the link is to be provided by an existential interpretation of the human situation. His program has been widely discussed. For this reason, as well as because the discussion has made it plain that his program is still not very clearly defined, I shall not attempt to discuss what might be involved in such an approach. Suffice it to say that the call for an existential prior understanding witnesses to the present need to take seriously the question of the relation of theology to experience. And, of course, it provides an approach to this question from which we shall hear a good deal more in the future.

IX

The Image of God

An understanding of human anxiety is of special relevance to the doctrine of man. Though it may not of itself establish, it does suggest a view of man's situation vis-à-vis God. Man's anxieties, particularly those which directly express a religious content, suggest that it is not correct simply to say man is separated from God by sin and death. Rather the situation appears to be more complex and dialectical. Man is threatened with separation. But he is aware of and anxious about the threat, anxious *because* he also feels that that which he is in danger of losing is good.

Do these considerations apply to all men? I would not deny that it is possible to conceive of a person who simply sins and feels no anxious guilt about it. In fact, the psychopath apparently fits this description. But in any case, I suggest that for the vast majority of mankind the descriptions of anxiety about guilt and death are applicable. Apparently, then, the experiences of anxiety suggest that, even for natural or "sinful" man, the positive bond between man and God is not severed. There appears to be, at least implicitly, a desire for God.

If, as I sought to establish in the preceding chapter, an understanding of experience is relevant to theology, it is clear, I think, that the theological significance of my inquiry into anxiety may be explored with reference to the doctrine of the image of God. This doctrine has a varied and complex history. But in all the various treatments of it one theme remains: man was created capable of and inclined to fellowship with God. In short, for Adam there was a desire for God which, with his creaturely endowments, he could express and satisfy. It is not my purpose here to undertake a full discussion, either historical or systematic, of this important doctrine. I hope, however, that I can suggest, with reference to it, what I meant by a concern to interpret experience mediating between opposing theologies.

In Chapter V, I discussed the opposing theologies. So far as the doctrine of the image of God is concerned, one theology, the Catholic, holds that the image of God is not destroyed or corrupted by the Fall of man and that it provides a basis for man's natural desire for God; the other, the Reformed, holds that the image of God is so radically defaced or corrupted that, though it may remain in substance, all its powers are lost.

Not only do these two theories stand in opposition to one another, but they have difficulty in remaining true to the Biblical view of man's relation to God. The Bible, not being concerned for "system," can present in almost dramatic form a view of man's situation which implies both his dignity and his wretchedness. The Bible relates our situation to that of Adam who was created good—in the image of God. Yet it also knows our need of a redeemer.

But consider the dilemma which seems to arise when we try to elaborate a doctrine of the image of God. There is a tendency either so to stress the image that it becomes incomprehensible why man should have to be redeemed at such cost, or so to negate the image that our relation to the good creation (Adam) is threatened. As I have suggested in discussing Barth, this latter tendency characterizes the Reformed tradition. The total depravity of man suggests simply that the image of God has been lost or destroyed. To say such a thing outright, however, would be to separate us entirely from man as created. We would become another species. And not only would the unity of history be destroyed, but it would become incomprehensible why we should suffer for Adam's sin. So Reformed theologians had to do a nimble dance to avoid saying that the image was totally lost and yet to avoid saying that any inclination toward God remained in man. The mystifying distinction between the substance and the powers of the image was employed to cover the confusion. Even so, it sometimes became evident, in the case of a theologian unafraid to speak clearly (such as Barth), that the nimble dancing was a failure. For, as I have argued (Ch. VIII), it became clear that our unity with Adam was denied anyway.

There is hope of resolving this dilemma, I believe, by approaching the concept of the image of God more dialectically. The retention of the image need not imply that man does not need to rely upon grace. But before developing this theme, I want to say a word about the other major historical tendency, that of Catholicism.

Catholicism protects our unity with Adam. He was created in the image of God. We retain the image, even after the Fall, though we have lost the "likeness to God," that is, our actual rectitude. The image of God in natural man is to be seen in the rational soul with its inclination to seek the good and its capacity to discern the good. As Luther pointed out (see p. 85), the tendency was to minimize the seriousness of sin, to make it seem reasonable that man could reach God without the intervention of divine grace.

It will very shortly be apparent that I wish to retain the concept of natural desire for God. But I am convinced that we need to think of this desire after a model quite different from that which dominated the imagination of scholastic theologians. As I pointed out in Chapter VI, they were dominated either by Aristotelian or Platonic models. The point that I wish to make here is that in either case the model tended to suggest that this natural desire is something that will fulfill itself with a minimum of conflict. It suggested an unfolding process in which no fundamental help from outside was needed. The Platonic imagination thought of the essence of the soul as being identical with the One which it naturally tended to rejoin. The Aristotelian model of natural desire is perhaps fundamentally biological—the acorn naturally tending toward its proper end, the oak.

There is nothing in these models to suggest a fundamental conflict in the expression of man's natural desire. If a man misses his proper end, it is due to an accident. In this case the concept of natural desire is not sufficiently dialectical. The natural course of love (desire) is smooth.

ANXIOUS DESIRE

In conclusion I wish to suggest that we think of man's desire for God after the model of that anxious desire whose nature has been the subject of this inquiry. The model is not the acorn growing to be an oak, but that anxious longing (Freud) which implies both a desire and a threat to its fulfillment. Along these lines we can, I think, make progress in resolving the dilemmas which have attached to more traditional approaches to the doctrine of the image of God. For it will not be necessary to think of the image as some kind of entity which is simply possessed or which has simply been lost. It can be thought of as a real but dynamic relation between tendencies inherent in human nature and the problematical fulfillment of those tendencies.

We have already seen that there is a similarity of structure between the anxiety described by Freud and that which emerges in religious experience. I am now suggesting that this similarity be made the basis of an analogy. Though I can hardly defend myself here, I believe there is an analogical element in every concept concerning God. To seek an analogy in our experience of anxiety is, I feel, not such a radical departure from tradition as might at first seem to be the case. Theologians have always used the analogy of love, and Jesus himself refers to the kind of love we experience in our families. Also, the experience of fear has often been used to express man's relation to God. Anxiety is very closely related to both of these. In fact, it is the experience in which love and fear are both held together in tension.

ANXIETY AND END POINTS OF DEVELOPMENT

The model which, I suggest, should guide our thinking is to be found in the work of Freud, though, so far as I know, he never explicitly gave it the formulation which I shall offer.[1]

Certain "end points of development" are laid down for the human individual in his very psychobiological nature. For Freud, heterosexual love is one such end point. That is, if a person does not continue to develop in the direction of a basically (though undoubtedly never perfect) heterosexual orientation to life, then violence is done to his nature in such a way that the person becomes psychologically ill. The evidence for this is the clinical data which reveal various kinds of crippling and painful symptoms connected with blockages in the developmental process. Further evidence, this time from the patient himself, consists in the judgment of those who have been to some degree liberated or healed by therapy that their former state was indeed a sickness.

I admit that this concept of an end point of development opens up debatable questions. For example, it implies a human nature in a nonrelativistic sense. That is, it implies that certain needs are given for the whole species. Just as the species needs food, without which it would perish, so there are psychic needs which are just as definite, though our understanding of them may not be so far advanced. Also, I am aware that I have not adequately described what Freud means by heterosexual love. An attempted description would take us far afield. Suffice it to say that he does not mean to confine this concept to the physical sex act between male and female. It has also, for example, to do with the capacity for object love, the capacity to give freely of oneself for the sake of the loved object. The loved object may be a person of the opposite sex or an ideal or a social movement.

The concept of an end point of development may be debatable, though I feel it can be convincingly defended. But it is a concept with deep roots in the Freudian understanding of man, in the light of which Freud's concept of anxious longing must be seen.

What shall we say, from the Freudian point of view, of these end points of development? Are they part of man? If so, where do they reside—in which faculty or part of the personality? If we cannot locate such an end point *in* man, must we say that man does not in any sense have it? Attempts to discuss this notion in terms of a faculty or entity of any kind, which may or may not be simply possessed, are fruitless. They do not get at the situation which the notion refers to. The situation is dynamic, developmental. It must be seen in terms of dynamic relations, not in terms of entities with given qualities.

The end of heterosexual love is *in* man (immanent) in the sense that his nature, with its given biological and psychological structure, as it develops exercises a kind of demand that this end be realized. The demand springs from his nature but also from the character of the relations which the individual experiences with persons and other realities outside himself. That is to say, love is a polar term, with reference, on the one hand, to certain psychobiological processes centered in the self and, on the other hand, to changing and developing relations to realities beyond the self. One might paraphrase Martin Buber and say that love is *between* the I and the Thou.

The end of heterosexual love is also *beyond* man (transcendent) in the sense that this demand of his nature can only be fulfilled in an other. Furthermore, the other is one over whom the self does not exercise complete control. Indeed, to the extent that the other is controlled, the relationship of love is destroyed. Freud is quite clear that love is a giving of the self in accordance with the needs of the beloved. The end is also transcendent in the empirical sense that there is a lot of evidence that no human being ever completely achieves it. To some extent the remnants of infantile and narcissistic restrictions remain with any individual. Yet to the extent that they do, a further demand is exercised in the direction of the end.

Two other points are important for my model or analogy. First, anxiety is precisely the sign of a tension between the demand which the end exercises and some threat to its fulfillment. In the case of Hans (see above pp. 52-53 ff.) the *sine qua non* of his anxiety was love for the mother; but this love or longing became anxious because of a threat to its fulfillment. Thus anxiety testifies to the fact that the individual is betwixt and between; that he is pulled in two directions. The pull toward the end which is desired is active, but it is in battle with an impediment. Anxiety is a sign that love is very much alive, but also that it is blocked.

Second, the removal of the blockage, the creative overcoming of anxiety, is not just an achievement of the individual. Even though we have the concept of an end point of development which exercises a demand over the individual, there is no suggestion that the demanded development will automatically take place. On the contrary, Freud and his followers seem to be very much aware of the precarious nature of the development of mature love. And this is so partly because we are dependent upon others in this matter. Once a blockage occurs, as it surely does with all people, its removal depends upon something analogous to the Christian concept of grace, that is, upon understanding and acceptance by others. This fact shows up clearly, for example, in the therapeutic process by which an attempt is made to overcome the blockage. No progress can be made in this process unless and until (and to the extent that) rapport and transference take place. That is the patient must come to feel that he is accepted by the therapist. He must find, in this relationship, grace—an understanding and acceptance which he cannot demand by right and which are given in spite of all the things about himself which he feels to be unacceptable. But this is true not only in formal therapy. The proper development of the individual depends at every stage upon his receiving from others something which cannot be demanded—their love and acceptance.

THE IMAGE OF GOD: NATURE AND GRACE

The experience of religious anxiety, with its implicit or explicit desire for God and also with its fear of separation from God, suggests that the above model or analogy may be applicable to the doctrine of the image of God. I say "suggests" rather than "demonstrates," for it is of course true that other considerations must be borne in mind, such as consistency with the crucial experiences in the formation and self-understanding of the community of faith. Yet, I believe, the suggestion becomes even more impressive when these considerations are borne in mind. The goodness of God's creation and providence, and man's need for and experience of redemption, are central to the Christian self-understanding. Neither element can be neglected. Yet, I am convinced, the major traditional formulations of the doctrine of the image of God do threaten one or another of these central Christian affirmations. The notion that man simply possesses the image threatens to minimize his need of redemption. The notion that the image has been lost, or rendered totally inefficacious, tends to place in question the goodness of creation—or, more usually, it tends to sever fallen man from Adam. It is necessary for the sake of Christian doctrine itself to construe the image of God in a more dialectical way—in a way which does justice both to man's unity with the goodness of creation and to his need for divine grace.

The model which I have suggested is, I think, able to help in this direction. It has the merit not only of avoiding overly simple alternatives (that man is good or that he is depraved) but of providing an analogue in common experience of that relationship which we believe to obtain between God and man. The belief is not, then, an arbitrary dogmatic interpretation of certain crucial experiences which happened a long time ago, but it is a belief illuminated by a prior understanding available to any man who reflects upon the significance of his anxieties.

First, then, man reflects the image of God by nature. That is to say, the image of God, man's capacity for and inclination to fellowship with God, is grounded in human nature. Just as, in the model suggested above, the end points of development are determined by man's psychobiological constitution, so man's spiritual end is determined by the way in which he has been created. "Thou has made us for Thyself. . . ."

Ultimately, of course, this situation is a reflection of grace. That is, according to Christian belief, all nature, including human nature, is a reflection of God's grace. God need not have so made us, but He freely chose to make us for Himself.

I have argued that the only theological reason for rejecting the present efficacy of the image of God, construed as a natural inclination toward God, is to protect the conviction that we stand in need of the special grace of Christ, the Redeemer. But here again, I think, our model may help us to avoid rushing to the alternative of total depravity, which raises more problems than it solves. The fact that certain end points of development are determined by man's nature does not prevent him from needing an acceptance and understanding from beyond himself—needing something which his own nature cannot possibly supply. So too in the spiritual realm, though man is never bereft of an inclination toward God (however unconscious it may be), he is not able of himself to fulfill this inclination. He needs divine grace, forgiveness, and acceptance.

Man's natural tendency toward heterosexual love is there, but it is threatened from many sides. It is in fact precarious and in all normal experience blocked and perverted to some degree. This blockage need not be regarded lightly. Nor, in the spiritual realm, need man's sin and its effects be lightly treated.

Just as man's psychological anxiety in general is the mark of the struggle between the inclination toward his proper end and the threats to such a fulfillment, so his religious anxiety is the mark of the struggle between our created end of fellowship with God and the many threats to its fulfillment. But so long as the anxiety is present, it witnesses not only to the threats and defeats but to the still living power of our desire for God.

In our common experience, anxiety is by no means always overcome. The threats and blockages may remain throughout life, and no doubt they ordinarily do to a considerable degree. Or, indeed, the desire for one's true end may be completely overwhelmed. But when that happens, the characteristic anxiety disappears. In the psychological realm, one then has the catatonic state of complete passivity. In the religious realm, one then has not anxiety but despair, the sickness unto death.

I am not trying, therefore, just to be optimistic. The battle, of which anxiety is the sign, is a mortal combat. If it issues in victory and life, it will be as a result of powerful aid from beyond the self. It will be because of grace. But so long as the battle rages, death has not yet won.

Throughout my argument, I have tried to show that anxiety is a phenomenon of love. Without love, or desire for what is felt to be good, anxiety could not arise. But if anxiety is the child of love, it is of a love which is embattled, whose end is far from secured, whose end indeed cannot by one's own power be secured.

Something ineradicable in man's nature, the image of God, calls him to that life of love and adoration which he has glimpsed again and again in his religious contemplation, and the glory of which has burst upon him in the person of Christ. But that life demands a selflessness which is frightening to mortal man. In his anxiety he "grasps at finiteness." The way is blocked by his own fearfulness. Yet the way of retrenchment, of seeking security in the finite, of sin, leaves him no rest. It is attended by anxiety which is the symptom both of the blockage and of his continuing need to move beyond it. This, I believe, is the human situation as it is to be seen in the light of our understanding of anxiety. And perhaps all that I have said is but a footnote to St. Augustine:

Thou has made us for Thyself, and our hearts are restless till they rest in Thee.

Notes

CHAPTER I. THE PRESENT SITUATION IN THEOLOGY

   1. John Bunyan, *Pilgrim's Progress* (London: Dent, 1904), pp. 181-82.

   2. Basel: Schwabe and Co., 1919, pp. 264-67.

   3. New York: Harper Torchbooks, 1957.

   4. *Ibid.*, pp. xxv, xxix, and xxx.

   5. See Karl Barth, *Die Protestantische Theologie im 19. Jahrhundert*, p. 411. See also his *Church Dogmatics*, tr. Thomson (New York: Scribner's, 1936), Vol. I, pt. 1, pp. 226 ff.

   6. See my article, "The Meaning of Religious Experiences," *Journal of Religion*, Vol. XXXII (1952), 263-71.

   7. William James, *The Varieties of Religious Experience* (New York: Longmans, Green, 1917), especially pp. 24-25.

CHAPTER II. THE WAY OF FEAR: ANXIETY IN TERESA OF ÁVILA

   1. One of the briefer yet excellent biographies of Teresa is found in René Fülop-Müller's *The Saints That Moved the World* (New York: Crowell, 1946).

For a longer treatment, see Marcelle Auclair, *Saint Teresa of Ávila* (New York: Pantheon, 1953).

Best of all, consult Teresa's own writings. St. Teresa of Ávila, *The Complete Works of Teresa of Jesus*, translated from the critical edition of Silverio and edited by E. A. Peers (New York: Sheed and Ward, 1946), 3 vols. (Referred to hereafter as *Works*.)

   2. *Works*, I, 85.

   3. This claim may be checked in a rewarding way: by

reading Teresa's writings, especially her *Life* and her *Interior Castle*, both contained in the *Works*. I have myself presented a more extensive analysis of Teresa's "way of fear" in my unpublished doctoral dissertation, "The Meaning of Religious Anxiety," University of Chicago, 1954.

4. James Leuba, *The Psychology of Religious Mysticism* (New York: Harcourt, Brace, 1926).

5. *Works*, I, 11.

6. *Ibid.*, I, 19. (Italics mine.)

7. *Ibid.*, I, 26.

8. *Ibid.*, I, 22.

9. *Ibid.*, I, 29.

10. *Ibid.*, I, 30.

11. *Ibid.*, I, 31.

12. *Ibid.*, I, 18, 23.

13. *Ibid.*, I, 23.

14. *Ibid.*, II, 126 ff.

15. *Ibid.*, I, 83-84, 90.

16. *Ibid.*, I, 40.

17. *Ibid.*, I, 45.

18. *Ibid.*, I, 48.

19. *Ibid.*, I, 53.

20. *Ibid.*, I, 54.

21. *Ibid.*, II, 235.

22. *Ibid.*, I, 163.

23. *Ibid.*, I, 162.

24. Teresa's account, Chaps. XXIII-XXVII of her *Life*, leaves the chronology uncertain.

25. *Works*, I, 164.

26. See *Ibid.*, I, 196.

27. *Ibid.*, I, 155.

28. *Ibid.*, II, 172 ff. *Et passim.*

29. *Ibid.*, I, 190.

30. *Ibid.*, I, 330-31.

31. *Ibid.*, I, 191.

32. *Ibid.*, I, 192-93.

33. *Ibid.*, II, 275-77.

34. *Ibid.*, II, 324.

35. St. John of the Cross, *The Ascent of Mount Carmel,* tr. D. Lewis (London: Thomas Baker, 1906), p. 61.

36. *Works,* II, 327-28.

37. *Ibid.,* II, 219 (Italics mine.)

38. See the recent treatment of this theme by John Dillenberger, *God Hidden and Revealed* (Philadelphia: Muhlenberg, 1953).

CHAPTER III. THE STRANGE WORK OF GOD: LUTHER'S INTERPRETATION OF ANXIETY

1. References to Luther are cited from the Weimar edition. "TR" refers to the *Tischreden;* "TR 2" would be Volume 2 of the *Tischreden;* "3, 424, 10" would be Volume 3 of the main works, page 424, section 10. Occasionally a volume is split into two parts, in which case the part is cited by a roman numeral (I or II) after the first arabic numeral.

2. This is perhaps an exaggeration in view of the fact that we do not have in his case anything like the abundance of clearly autobiographical material bearing upon this problem that we find in the case of Teresa. Luther's comments on anxiety are more scattered, less systematic. Yet he regards anxiety as so important that he says it is impossible to learn true theology without it (43, 472, 18). "If I were to live long enough, I would write a book about *Anfechtung,* without which nobody can understand the Scriptures or know the fear and love of God, nay, he cannot know what the Spirit is" (TR 4, 4777).

3. A good discussion of the impossibility of a psychological reconstruction is given in Gordon Rupp, *The Righteousness of God* (New York: Philosophical Library, 1953), pp. 83-87.

4. For example, P. Bühler, *Die Anfechtung bei Martin Luther* (Zürich: Zwingli-Verlag, 1942); G. Jacob, *Der Gewissensbegriff in der Theologie Luthers* (Tübingen: 1929); E. Vogelsang, *Der Angefochtene Christus bei Luther* (Berlin: 1932); F. K. Schumann, *Gottesglaube und Anfechtung bei Luther* (Leipzig: 1938).

5. In common usage the term referred usually to a physical attack of some kind, but before Luther's time it had been used

in the religious sense by Meister Eckhardt and Johann Tauler, the latter of whom is recognized by Luther as influencing him on this point (1, 557, 26).

6. Hereafter, I shall use the word "anxiety" to refer to this terrible awareness of *Anfechtungen*.

7. See Bühler, *op. cit.*, pp. 192 ff.

CHAPTER IV.   ANXIOUS LONGING: FREUD'S INTERPRETATION OF ANXIETY

1. I shall assume without argument, though a good argument could be made, that Freud is not only representative of the best psychological work in this area but that most modern work rests upon his fundamental discoveries.

2. S. Freud, *The Problem of Anxiety*, tr. H. A. Bunker (New York: Norton, 1936), pp. 74-75, 93 ff.

3. *Ibid.*, pp. 71-73.

4. S. Freud, *A General Introduction to Psychoanalysis*, tr. J. Rivière (Garden City, N.Y.: Permabooks, 1953), p. 404.

5. Freud, *The Problem of Anxiety*, p. 70; see also p. 21.

6. *Ibid.*, p. 81.

7. This case is presented in S. Freud, *Collected Papers*, tr. J. Rivière (New York: International Psycho-analytic Press, 1924-50), Vol. III, and it is reviewed in connection with Freud's concept in *The Problem of Anxiety*.

8. Freud, "Analysis of a Phobia in a Five-Year-Old Boy," *loc. cit.*, III, 166.

9. *Ibid.*, pp. 167-69. (Italics mine.)

10. Freud, *The Problem of Anxiety*, p. 87.

11. *Ibid.*, p. 113.

12. S. Freud, *New Introductory Lectures on Psychoanalysis*, tr. W. J. H. Sprott (New York: Norton, 1933), p. 115.

13. Freud, *The Problem of Anxiety*, p. 80.

14. Freud, *New Introductory Lectures*, p. 120. See also *The Problem of Anxiety*, p. 39.

15. Freud, *The Problem of Anxiety*, p. 65.

16. *Ibid.*, p. 86.

17. *Ibid.*, p. 87.

18. *Ibid.*, p. 114.

19. *Ibid.*, p. 112.

20. *Ibid.*, p. 67.

21. *Ibid.*, p. 78.

22. *Ibid.*, p. 75.

23. *Ibid.*, pp. 78-79.

24. Freud, *A General Introduction to Psychoanalysis*, p. 424.

25. *Ibid.*, p. 422.

26. Freud, *A General Introduction to Psychoanalysis*, pp. 424-25.

CHAPTER V.   THE SCHOOL OF ANXIETY

1. My own extended interpretation of Kierkegaard on this point is given in my unpublished dissertation, University of Chicago, 1954.

2. Søren Kierkegaard, *The Concept of Dread*, tr. W. Lowrie (Princeton: Princeton University Press, 1944), p. 38.

3. *Ibid.*, p. 52.

4. Søren Kierkegaard, *The Sickness unto Death*, tr. W. Lowrie (Princeton: Princeton University Press, 1941), pp. 18-19.

5. *Ibid.*, p. 55.

6. Kierkegaard, *The Concept of Dread*, The forms of anxiety which result from sin are discussed in Chaps. III-IV.

7. *Ibid.*, p. 139.

8. *Ibid.*, p. 143.

9. Kierkegaard, *The Sickness unto Death*.

10. Martin Heidegger, *Sein und Zeit* (2nd ed., Halle: Max Niemeyer Verlag, 1929), pp. 183-84. When a quotation from *Sein und Zeit* is given in English, the translation is mine.

11. *Ibid.*, p. 1.

12. *Ibid.*, pp. 19 ff.

13. Martin Heidegger, *Existence and Being*, tr. Scott, Hull, and Crick, Introduction by Werner Brock (Chicago: Regnery, 1949), p. 380.

14. Heidegger, *Sein und Zeit*, pp. 4-5.

15. In the following analysis I shall use the term "man" to

translate Heidegger's technical *Dasein*. Strictly speaking, this is not precise; for "man" is too much of an abstraction. By *Dasein* Heidegger wishes to suggest the concrete way of being-in-the-world which characterizes the human individual. Nevertheless, I think it advisable to avoid a word which is bound to be a blank to the average reader.

16. Martin Heidegger, *Platons Lehre von der Wahrheit, mit einem Brief über den Humanismus* (Bern: Francke, 1947), p. 54.

17. "Das Sein deises Seinden ist je meines." Heidegger, *Sein und Zeit*, p. 41.

18. "Das 'Wesen' des Daseins liegt in seiner Existenz." *Ibid.*, p. 42.

19. *Ibid.*, pp. 42-43.

20. *Ibid.*, pp. 12-13.

21. *Ibid.*, p. 71.

22. *Ibid.*, p. 145.

23. *Ibid.*, p. 12.

24. *Ibid.*, p. 192.

25. *Ibid.*, p. 192.

26. *Ibid.*, p. 118.

27. *Ibid.*, pp. 42-43.

28. *Ibid.*, pp. 134 ff.

29. *Ibid.*, p. 187.

30. *Ibid.*, *passim*, especially pp. 184 ff. We will return once again to his detailed analysis of anxiety.

31. *Ibid.*, pp. 235 ff.

32. *Ibid.*, pp. 252 ff.

33. *Ibid.*, p. 184.

34. *Ibid.*, p. 186.

35. *Ibid.*

36. *Ibid.*

37. *Ibid.*, p. 189.

38. *Ibid.*, p. 187.

39. *Ibid.*

40. *Ibid.*, p. 235.

41. Heidegger, *Existence and Being*, p. 370.

42. *Ibid.*, p. 369.

43. *Ibid.*, p. 383.

44. *Ibid.*, pp. 384-85.

45. *Ibid.*, p. 369.

46. Martin Heidegger, *Erläuterungen zu Hölderlins Dichtung* (Frankfurt am Main: Klostermann, 1951), pp. 9-30.

47. "Furchtlos bleibt aber, so er muss, der Mann Einsam vor Gott, es shützet die Einfalt ihn, Und Keiner Waffen braucht's und keiner Listen, so lange, bis Gottes Fehl hilft." *Ibid.*, p. 27.

CHAPTER VI.   CONFLICTING INTERPRETATIONS

1. *On the Trinity*, tr. A. Haddan (Edinburgh: T. and T. Clark, 1873), Book XI, Chap. 5.

2. A good summary of the Catholic discussion of this concept is to be found in Antoninus Finili, O.P., "Natural Desire," *Dominican Studies*, I (1948), 313-59.

3. Thomas Aquinas, *Summa Theologica*, tr. Dominican Fathers (London: Washbourne, 1912), I, 93, a.4.

4. *Ibid.*

5. *Ibid.*, II-I, 85, a.1.

6. *Ibid.*, I, 95, a.1.

7. *Ibid.*, II-I, 85, a.1.

8. *Ibid.*

9. *Ibid.*, II-I, 2, a.8.

10. *Ibid.*, II-I, 109-14.

11. Thomas Aquinas, *Summa Contra Gentiles*, Book III, Part 1, tr. by V. Bourke (Garden City: Doubleday, 1956), Chap. 16.

12. *Ibid.*, Chap. 17.

13. *Ibid.*, Chap. 19. The reference in quotation marks is to Aristotle, *Nicomachean Ethics*, IX, 7.

14. Augustine, *Confessions*, tr. F. J. Sheed (New York: Sheed and Ward, 1943), Book I, Chap. 1.

15. Augustine, *On the Trinity*, Book VIII, Chap. 2; Book XIV, Chap. 14.

16. *Ibid.*, Book VIII, Chap. 3.

17. *Ibid.*, Book X.

18. *Ibid.*, Book X, Chap. 5; Book XIV, Chaps. 7-8.

19. *Ibid.*, Book XI, Chaps. 5-8; Book XV, Chap. 22.

20. Augustine, *Confessions*, Book XIII, Chaps. 9-10. See also *The City of God*, tr. M. Dods (Edinburgh: T. and T. Clark, 1871), Book XI, Chap. 28.

21. Augustine, *Soliloquys*, tr. T. Gilligan (New York: Cosmopolitan Science and Art Service Co., 1943), Book I, Chap. 1.

22. Augustine, *On the Happy Life*, tr. L. Schopp (St. Louis: Herder, 1939), Book II, Chaps. 8-11.

23. Augustine, *The City of God*, Book XII, Chap. 1.

24. F. D. E. Schleiermacher, *The Christian Faith*, tr. Mackintosh and Stewart (Edinburgh: T. and T. Clark, 1928), p. 22.

25. *Ibid.*, p. 54.

26. *Ibid.*, pp. 54-55.

27. *Ibid.*, p. 277.

28. Martin Luther, "Selected Psalms," *Luther's Works*, tr. J. Pelikan and others (St. Louis: Concordia, 1955), Vol. XII, p. 308.

29. *Ibid.*, p. 307.

30. John Calvin, *Institutes of the Christian Religion*, tr. J. Allen (Philadelphia: Presbyterian Board of Education, 1816), Book II, Chap. 2, sec. 27.

31. Heinrich Heppe, *Reformed Dogmatics*, ed. Bizer, tr. Thomson (London: Allen and Unwin, 1950), p. 520. It is interesting that this work was "rediscovered" by Karl Barth, who writes a Foreword to the present edition.

32. Calvin, *op. cit.*, Book II, Chap. 2, sec. 27.

33. John Knox, "The Confession of Faith," Chap. III in *John Knox's History of the Reformation in Scotland*, ed. W. C. Dickinson (New York: Philosophical Library, 1950), Vol. II.

34. *Ibid.*, Chap. XII.

35. Karl Barth, *Die Kirchliche Dogmatik* (Zürich: Evangelischer Verlag Ag. Zollikon, 1953), IV, 1. Section 60 contains Barth's discussion of man as sinner. He makes it quite plain that man's depravity is "total" (p. 555). "There can be no talk of a good 'kernel' within man which is somehow untouched by his evil" (p. 551). Where an English quotation from this volume is given, the translation is mine.

36. *Ibid.*, IV, 1, pp. 395 ff. For example, see p. 533: "The

self-understanding in which man recognizes himself as sinner and as fallen, can only be the self-understanding of the man who hears and believes God's Word: the man who takes upon himself and acknowledges God's judgment and sees himself in the light of this judgment. No self-understanding won in any other way can be an introduction to this self-understanding."

37. *Ibid.*, p. 532. "No one understands by his own insight that he is fallen."

38. *Ibid.*, p. 537.

39. *Ibid.*, I, 2, sec. 17, 2, contains Barth's discussion of "religion as unbelief."

40. *Ibid.*, IV, 1, p. 397.

41. *Ibid.*, pp. 682-84. This is a free rendition of the gist of a long, complex characterization of the recognition, possible only in faith, of the insecurity of all human efforts to gain security.

42. *Ibid.*, pp. 531 ff.

43. *Ibid.*, p. 399.

CHAPTER VII. THEOLOGY AND EXPERIENCE

1. In citing their work with approval, however, I do not wish to imply that I accept their narrowing of the concept "experience" to "sense experience." This is justified only so long as the talk is of the natural sciences. I have suggested elsewhere that even the positivists, who have certainly demonstrated that science does rely upon the order of experience, face difficulties in stating with precision or adequacy how science and experience are related. See "Logical Empiricism and Philosophical Theology," *The Journal of Religion*, XXXV (Oct., 1955), pp. 207-17.

2. John Wisdom, "Gods," *New Essays in Philosophical Theology*, ed. Flew and MacIntyre (New York: Macmillan, 1955).

3. Albert Einstein and Leopold Infeld, *The Evolution of Physics* (New York: Simon and Schuster, 1938), p. 310.

4. For a discussion of these matters, as well as a number of related ones, see C. G. Hempel, "Fundamentals of Concept

Formation in Empirical Science," *International Encyclopedia of Unified Science* (Chicago: University of Chicago Press, 1952), Vol. II, No. 7.

5. I have discussed these matters more fully in "Logical Empiricism and Philosophical Theology." I believe that my distinction between scientific and philosophic considerations is similar to that made by so-called linguistic analysts. See Gilbert Ryle, *Dilemmas* (Cambridge, Eng.: Cambridge University Press, 1954), p. 5.

6. See, for example, Hempel, *op. cit.*

7. On this point see the cogent criticism of Barth in Gustaf Wingren, *Theology in Conflict* (Philadelphia: Muhlenberg, 1958), especially pp. 31-35.

8. In this sense Archimedes' principle saves the appearance in connection with our experiences of things floating or sinking in water.

9. Wingren, *op. cit.*, p. 32.

10. *Ibid.*, p. 35.

11. These distinctions are discussed in H. Heppe, *Reformed Dogmatics*, tr. by G. T. Thomson (London: Allen and Unwin, 1950), pp. 361 ff.

CHAPTER VIII.   ANXIETY AND THE WORD: THE POSITION OF KARL BARTH

1. See above, p. 15.

2. See Barth's *Church Dogmatics*, tr. G. T. Thomson (New York: Scribner's, 1936), Vol. I, pt. 2, sec. 13, 1, but especially pp. 7 ff.

3. *Ibid.*, Vol. I, pt. 1, p. 227.

4. One could conceive of a theology as barren as possible of all interpretation. Such a theology would have to consist of various devices for "pointing to" whatever events are regarded as crucial in God's confronting of us. Poets and mystics struggle with the problem of pointing us to events or things of which no adequate interpretation can be given. But I frankly think there is nothing we as humans can do to point to particular events (especially since our pointing is, in theology, through language)

without at the same time giving some interpretation of them. If our theology really depends upon a totally passive relation to the revealing events, we have to say that only God Himself can point to the crucial events. Then we either have to be silent (Oh, blessed respite from books of theology!) or to assume that in at least some books of theology the Holy Ghost is the author. This leaves no human criterion for deciding which books had better been left unwritten. In this problem, as in all others, Barth's position drives us to a monism in which God is all, and man and history ultimately nothing.

5. On this point see Richard R. Niebuhr, *The Resurrection and Historical Reason* (New York: Scribner's, 1957), pp. 46-51.

6. See the passage cited on p. 121 above.

7. In his analysis Niebuhr shows why, for Barth, the revealing event is essentially an historical. See *op. cit.*, pp. 46-51. An even sharper criticism of Barth, which shows his conflict with the Biblical point of view, and which also charges him with negating the significance of history, is to be found in Wingren, *op. cit.*

8. Barth, *Church Dogmatics*, tr. G. T. Thomson (New York: Scribner's, 1936), Vol. I, pt. 1, p. 227.

9. *Ibid.*, p. 229.

10. Thomas Aquinas, *Summa Theologica*, II-I, 109-14.

11. Rudolf Bultmann, *Essays* (New York: Macmillan, 1955), pp. 257-58. (Italics his.)

12. *Ibid.*, pp. 259 ff.

13. *Ibid.*, p. 252. (Italics his.)

14. *Ibid.*, p. 253. (Italics his.)

15. *Ibid.*, p. 256.

16. *Ibid.*, p. 257. (Italics his.) The quotation from Augustine is the familiar "Thou hast made us for Thyself, and our hearts are restless till they rest in Thee."

CHAPTER IX. THE IMAGE OF GOD

1. The formulation given here is more closely approximated in Leon Saul, *Emotional Maturity* (Philadelphia: Lippincott, 1947). I am indebted even more, however, to my colleague, Professor F. W. Gramlich.

Index

157